WITHDRAWN

Brand New.

To Dornie

Wally Olins.
Brand New.

The Shape of Brands to Come.

30 illustrations in black and white

 Thames & Hudson

Brand New: The Shape of Brands to Come © 2014
Wally Olins

Designed by Daren Cook

Typeset in Enigma 2, designed by Jeremy Tankard

First published in 2014 in paperback in the United
States of America by Thames & Hudson Inc.,
500 Fifth Avenue, New York, New York 10110

thamesandhudsonusa.com

Library of Congress Catalogue Card Number
2013950846

ISBN 978-0-500-29139-9

Printed and bound in China by Everbest Printing Co. Ltd

Contents

Introduction.
Brands and Branding in the Future.

What is going to happen to brands and branding? Is it all over? Does globalization mean that variety and individuality will be crushed out of existence by massive multinational corporations who will dominate world markets with their immense promotional power? Does it mean that, wherever we live, we will all end up buying and using versions of the same stuff? Will everywhere in the world become increasingly similar, like airports today?

If, on the other hand, globalization is taking over and the world is becoming increasingly homogenous, how is it that nation, region and city branding have become so important? Why is every place shouting so loudly that it is the most attractive spot in the world to invest in and to visit, and that the brands it produces are the world's most desirable? If everything and everywhere is becoming increasingly similar, will there still be room for places that trade on being different?

Or is something completely different happening? Does the rise of digital technology mean that corporations will increasingly be on the defensive because customers will not only answer back but will ask a few questions and make a few demands on their own initiative? Does digital mean that everyone who feels like it will be able to make their own brand and market it – like self-publishing? And, if it does, where does that leave the multinational corporation?

What do we customers want anyway? Do we want it cheap? Do we want it authentic? Do we want it, whatever it is, to come from 'somewhere' – place branding again? Do we want it all at the same time? Or do we just keep changing our minds on alternate Thursdays?

What about sustainability, going green, global warming, the environment, and so on? How do they affect the way we think about the products and services we consume? And how do they influence the way we feel about the organizations that make and sell those products and services? Do we really believe that oil companies want to save the world? Is corporate social responsibility (CSR) as significant as everybody now says, or is it just a shibboleth or even a passing fad? And how can companies reconcile maximizing profitability with CSR?

Put another way, what is the corporation there for? To make profit and grow, or to help society, or both? And how can the corporation demonstrate that it cares – if it cares? And what if it operates through a multiplicity of brands? Does this mean that the corporation has to stand up and be counted; that it has to be seen to be the face behind all its brands? What about charities and NGOs? Are they going to become more professional and brand themselves?

Then there is the changing shape of world power; the relative decline of the West in the face of the growing political and economic power of emerging markets. Or do we mean already emerged markets? Will these countries start producing and promoting global brands based around their own cultural strengths and heritage? And, if they do, what will this mean for the traditional global dominance of brands based around Western cultural norms? Will they die, or will there just be more competition?

And then, assuming for the moment that brands don't die and that there will always be plenty of them around, who's going to build and sustain them? And what will happen to the brand consultancy business? Will it increasingly rely on metrics, quantification and 'scientific' research? What about flair and intuition in the creation and sustainability of brands? Will this disappear and be replaced by bland work created entirely out of 'rigorous' analysis? Put another way, will there be yet another face-off between rational and emotional; rigour and intuition; head and heart?

All these, and a few other issues, too, face the branding activity over the next decades. I am writing about it all now, because I won't be here to see it and listen to people telling me how wrong I was.

Wally Olins, Goring-on-Thames, 2013

1

The New Authenticity.

I am getting a bit bored of reading about whether the Mini is still authentically British. The Mini is built in Oxford, the Rolls-Royce is put together at Goodwood; both are owned by BMW and, if you look carefully, it shows. But, of course, both want to say they are British. Maybe they are, but they certainly have a strong German accent. Bentley, assembled at Crewe and owned by VW, isn't that British either. It's full of the same parts as VW's prestige car, the Phaeton. Is Jaguar Land Rover, owned by Tata, still British? The point about all these cars is that they try, and they sort of seem, to be British. They certainly emphasize heritage.

What about the Peugeot 107 and Citroën C1? Are they French? Is the Toyota Aygo Japanese? They are all more or less the same car underneath, and they are all built in the Czech Republic … in the same factory.

Some true blue British cars made by Aston Martin – a
company, incidentally, owned by a Kuwaiti consortium and
run by a German – are built in Austria. Nobody talks about that.
Slovakia makes more cars per head than any other country in
the world, but nobody talks about that either.

In an era in which transnational companies are making
everything everywhere, at a point in time when nobody really
knows where most things come from, we, as consumers, still
love to think that the things we treasure come from somewhere
– a particular place. We like to feel that provenance is a guarantor
of quality; that it confirms our preconceptions about German
technology, or Spanish passion, or Italian style, or French flair,
or perhaps more especially food from local ingredients – and
often it does. So perhaps, because almost everything we touch
comes from all over the globe, paradoxically this increases our
yearning for authenticity and provenance.

Just behind where I live in England's Thames Valley is a farm
which, in a very short season, grows asparagus. As soon as the
season begins, we rush over and pick as much as we can and we
have lots of friends over to eat it. Then we casually say, 'Do you
like the asparagus? We picked it yesterday in the field just over
there. Yes, it's real Oxfordshire asparagus.' Of course, they all love
it. It's the authenticity that gets them. It's local and it's fresh
and we picked it with our own hands. And everyone feels good
about it, because it didn't burn up carbon to get here and it's
sustainable and environmentally friendly and all the other
good things you can think of.

So, where we can, we continually emphasize provenance.
Our supermarkets and specialist food shops are full of products
whose provenance is its main differentiator: fruit, cheese, beef,

lamb, pork, poultry, soap, cosmetics, everything – 'Grown in...', or made using ingredients 'grown in...'.

Then there are the farmers' markets, bringing fruit, vegetables, fish and meat straight from the countryside to the urban customer. Of course, you expect these in small country towns or even in some cities, but they are absolutely everywhere, every week. There's a farmers' market every Sunday just off smart, chic, bustling, trendy Marylebone High Street in central London, just a few blocks away from Selfridges department store ... and it's genuine. Then there's another, Borough Market, practically opposite the Tower of London. Borough Market is so famous – not just for its fresh food, but also for its cafés, pop-up restaurants and the rest of the foodie mix – that it's now a significant tourist attraction.

And it's not just London. And it's not just Britain. And it's not just Europe, or the United States (there's one in Santa Monica, right in the middle of the Los Angeles conurbation). In fact, one of the biggest and most seductive farmers' markets I have ever been to was in Fremantle in Western Australia.

Why are they so successful? Because they are authentic, or they seem to be. There doesn't appear to be any kind of barrier between us, the consumers, and the people who bring us the stuff. They grew it, or they caught it in the sea, or they reared it and butchered it, and now they stand behind a stall selling it. We know where it comes from, or we think we do. Authenticity means provenance. It not only tastes good but it gives us a feeling of well-being. We are doing the right thing, both for ourselves and for the planet.

Of course, authenticity has always been part of the mix that we consumers have wanted, but not like now. Something is

changing and some of us just can't get enough of it. It's the inevitable paradox: the more the world goes global, the more we prize the local and the authentic ... or what we assume to be the authentic. This is a trend that's been spotted, mostly by small, entrepreneurial companies. The bigger companies, for the most part, have been caught napping.

Just take cereals, for instance. I have in front of me, as I write, two packs of breakfast cereals, Kellogg's and Dorset Cereals. The Kellogg's packaging is a classic traditional example of fast moving consumer goods (FMCG) branding – noisy, brash, full of exaggerated claims, repetitive, almost clownish, but quite charming and of course very familiar to us. We all grew up with that kind of thing. *'Kellogg's – a source of vitamin D – helps to build strong bones'* repeated here and there a few times, together with a lot of similar stuff scattered all over the multicoloured packaging. Of course, the copy is a bit tendentious and misleading. It often is. That's part of the tradition.[1]

Next to it is Dorset Cereals – *'honest, tasty and real'* – in a sober dark brown carton. Dorset Cereals is also a classic example of packaging, but of the new wave. It is simple, almost austere, and understated. The copy is deliberately self-deprecating and it's quite witty, and the packaging silently screams authenticity and provenance.

Everywhere you look, in the food and drink world especially, you find it. Real beer is also making a comeback. Of course, the carbonated, sourish fluid that's produced all over the world still dominates the market, but, in the United States, Samuel Adams of Boston and hundreds of other small craft breweries are making a big impact. In London, Shoreditch Blonde and Camden Hell's Lager combine authenticity with provenance, and they both come from the heart of inner London where all the little design studios working on digital videogames live. Even potato chips, traditionally a snack loaded with every kind of synthetic and addictive nastiness, seem to have been influenced by the trend towards authenticity. It's all about being pure, using unadulterated ingredients and no e-numbers. Burts Potato Chips of Devon ('Naturally Delicious') apparently *'supplies the best Paris restaurants'*. I quote from their product description: *'down here in deepest Devon … [we] make fantastic chips using only the finest and freshest natural ingredients'*.

Authentic brands come from everywhere, but they have to be based around provenance. L'Occitane isn't just from France; it comes from a specific region – Provence. The L'Occitane website claims that the company's cosmetics and creams are made from locally sourced ingredients in the Manosque factory, which the founder rescued from ruins in the 1970s. Natural ingredients, traditional Provençal manufacturing methods and a passionate business owner, who claims he's still getting his hands dirty making soaps and gathering rosemary: that's what L'Occitane says it's about. And there are L'Occitane shops everywhere – in France, of course, but all over Europe, in the United States, in Turkey, all based around marketing products from a region in France that many customers will never have heard of, but nevertheless love the feeling of authenticity they get.

It's happening in clothes, too. Pringle of Scotland and all those 'Made in Italy' brands have been with us for years. Remarkably, perhaps, Prada of Italy seems to be going one stage further. Harking back to an earlier tradition, Prada proposes to produce designs *'utilizing the traditional craftsmanship, materials and manufacturing techniques of different regions'*. Its 'Made in ...' projects will feature local products with labels detailing the origin of each product.[2]

Most of the smallish, newish, innovative brands have also seen that authenticity is linked to charm. The language they use is informal and chatty. Here's just a sample from the drinks company Innocent:

- *'TM = Thanks Mate. (R) = rainbow (C) = cool.'*
- *'You should try opening this carton at the other end. Not that we're telling you how to run your life or anything but it seems to work much easier.'*
- *'Call us on the banana phone on 020 ...'*
- *'Shake before pouring. It helps if the cap's on.'*

• • •

Innocent packaging:
a cracking good read.

So what does this move towards authenticity, simplicity and charm mean? That the righteous and just are taking over the world and nobody is going to exaggerate anymore? That the longstanding tradition of the FMCG world, based around dissimulation and half-truths, is over? That globalization is finished and that everything will become local and artisanal? Hardly. Let's not get too excited. It's doubtful whether these new, authentic products have more than a tiny proportion of the marketplace so far. They appeal to a quite small, sophisticated audience over a relatively narrow range of products. But it's a market that's growing fast – and it's highly influential.

What we are beginning to see is a change in the spirit of our times, and it's gradually making an impact on our lives. It's a very complex and long-term trend that will affect different sectors of the market with different levels of emphasis at different times. Of course, as consumers, we are, as usual, trying to have it every way. We want it cheap and good value, especially in a time of profound economic unease and austerity: that's why the discounters such as Aldi and Lidl are so successful, and that's why Walmart is still the world's biggest supermarket group. We also want it now, immediately: so if it's flowers from Kenya and we live in London, we'll have to overlook that. But somewhere or other, right inside us, we also want it to be pure, honest and sustainable. And, if it's food particularly, we want to know what we're eating: we don't want it mucked up with additives. That's why Whole Foods Market of the United States is so successful.

But when this fundamental shift was first taking place, most of the big companies didn't even seem to notice. P&G, Coca-Cola, Pepsi and the others, with all their research and their focus groups and their scenario planning and the rest of their elaborate, complex, sophisticated forecasting techniques, were apparently oblivious to what was happening under their noses. Or, if they did notice or they were told, they did nothing about it. It took them years to take note that there was a major mood change and now, belatedly and clumsily, they are trying to catch up.

Big companies are often very bad at predicting change. They tend to insulate themselves from its realities. They are comfortable following, not leading. They grow by acquisition rather than by innovation. As the new, small, clever companies grow and become successful, they get bought by the clumsy giants. Coca-Cola now owns Innocent, and Pepsi owns Naked.

McDonald's is also lumbering into the authenticity marketplace. It's not as though it couldn't have guessed that something was coming. For years there have been articles, blogs and books attacking the company and its suppliers; there have even been court cases. And McDonald's seemed oblivious, almost blind, to what was going on. Or it went into denial and fought it, despite the plethora of warning signs. Then, slowly, McDonald's began to change. Its menus started to trumpet the virtues of simple, natural food. It began, belatedly, to adapt to what it believed were changing tastes and it bought into brands that it thought understood these changing tastes. It even began to turn some of its fascias green.

In 2001, McDonald's bought a chunk of Pret A Manger, the UK-based High Street café/takeaway group. Pret had built its entire reputation on fresh, authentic food. Needless to say, there were no McD golden arches to be seen on or near Pret establishments. Even so, it became clear that Pret and McDonald's didn't mix. Customers were uncomfortable that McDonald's was somehow involved. Apparently, Pret management didn't much like it either, so the brand was bought back and sold to someone else. Since then, McDonald's has been a bit more careful where it puts its giant feet.

This is just one example. You can find them everywhere. Both Coca-Cola and Pepsi are focusing on new 'healthy living' products. In 2008, Coca-Cola bought 40% of a company called Honest Tea; in 2011, it bought the rest. Coca-Cola's Glacéau Vitaminwater is imitating Innocent with wacky copy ('a bunch of nice guys making a cool product'), using phrases clearly adapted from the brands, such as Innocent, that it has bought.

And so are the others. It seems that the Good Life, authenticity, informality and charm are now on the corporate agenda. Pepsi has claimed that this is an outline of its strategy for 2015:[3]

- Eliminate the direct sale of full-sugar soft drinks to primary and secondary schools around the globe by 2012.
- Provide access to safe water to three million people in developing countries by the end of 2012.
- Increase the whole grains, fruits and vegetables, nuts, seeds and low-fat dairy in its product portfolio.

In other words, Pepsi wants to look more pure, authentic and charming, even a bit organic, and inevitably it's trying hard to act like a socially responsive and responsible corporation.

• • •

'Organic' is an interesting word. Somewhere, somehow or other, it has an emotional association with authenticity. Organic products have been around for a long time, certainly since the 1970s, when they were part of the territory occupied by 'simple lifers'. Organics only gradually became mainstream, and their growth had nothing to do with big companies: neither manufacturers nor retailers were initially interested. It was the 'beard and sandals' brigade who gradually pushed organics into the mainstream, and organics in turn influenced the mood towards authenticity.

There are lots of definitions of 'organic' on websites. None of them is really clear and specific. All we really know is that organic foods are supposed to be purer, more authentic you might say, and they cost more – and, sometimes, but not always, they are a bit more tasty. Certainly they make us feel better because we think we are doing the right thing by the planet. The definitions around organic products are vague, simply because the reality is vague too.

The Organic Trade Association says this on its website: '[Organic production is a] production system that is managed in accordance with the Act and regulations ... to respond to site-specific conditions by integrating cultural, biological, and mechanical practices that foster cycling of resources, promote ecological balance, and conserve biodiversity....

'... The principal guidelines for organic production are to use materials and practices that enhance the ecological balance of natural systems and that integrate the parts of the farming system into an ecological whole. Organic agriculture practices cannot ensure that products are completely free of residues; however, methods are used to minimize pollution from air, soil and water.' I hope you've got all that and that you're still following.

Here's another definition from the UK Government's Department for Environment, Food and Rural Affairs, in answer to the question 'What is organic food?': 'In one sense all food is organic, because it has come from plants or animals. However for some *fifty years the word organic has been used to describe food grown without most artificial fertilisers or pesticides and in a way that emphasises crop rotation, making the most of natural fertilisers and ensuring that the life of the soil is maintained. Animals are kept in ways which minimise the need for medicines and other chemical treatments.'* Well, that's a bit better.

The Soil Association puts it very simply: *'Our definition of organic food is food which is produced using environmentally and animal friendly farming methods on organic farms. These methods are legally defined and any food sold as "organic" must be strictly regulated.*

'Organic farming recognises the direct connection between our health and how the food we eat is produced. Artificial fertilisers are banned and farmers develop fertile soil by rotating crops and using compost, manure and clover.

'Organic animals enjoy the very highest welfare standards – they are truly free range and have plenty of space and access to fields....

'Organic standards are the rules and regulations that define how an organic product is made. This is laid down in European Union (EU) law.'

The truth seems to be that organics, whatever they may be, are about a feeling for authenticity and that we, the consumers, want them. Are we victims of the placebo effect? Maybe.

Our search for authenticity derives, in particular, from one of society's most significant current moods, which is the rejection of excess: too much sugar, too much salt, too much obesity, too much waste, too much consumerism and too much pretence (the pretence that something originates in a particular place when it doesn't; when it's a fake). As usual, the mood of the times is reflected in its art – so you could say too much post-modernism.

Now the ethos is: 'Put your waste in different bags and be serious about the environment, sustainability and your own well-being and, where you can, buy authentic.' Except maybe when it's cheap, glamorous and irresistible, like some of the clothes in Zara or H&M, or even Primark. Then we suddenly find we don't care all that much about provenance.

• • •

Authenticity is not a movement; it's not like Occupy. It's not anti-capitalist. It's not anti-anything, and it doesn't dominate our lives. It's one strand of several. It's for things that, in our hearts, we know are right – such as moderation and honesty. No group is behind it, but millions of individuals are driving it. It's a manifestation of the spirit of our times. And, somehow, we are all beginning to be influenced by it.

At last, 'authenticity' is beginning to have a significant impact on product brands and branding. Many big organizations are beginning to recognize the feeling for it all around them and they understand that they have to come to terms with it. Or, as a trendy young marketer I know put it: 'Authenticity is the new thing. Now we have to learn how to fake it.'

Of course, authenticity directly relates to, and is a manifestation of, the sustainability movement. Give or take a bit, some people in some places – an increasing number – are concerned about the major environmental issues. Is global warming a reality? Are we busily destroying our own environment? Are we ruining the planet for our children and grandchildren and their children?

The influence of this kind of thinking – well, in a sense, it's *feeling* rather than thinking – varies according to place, socio-economic class, age, nationality and a whole variety of other factors. But it's there, and it's growing, and it's having a profound effect on brands and branding and on the way corporations behave or want to be seen to behave.

What is the shift of emphasis to authenticity all about? Is it just a passing fad, or a really significant mood change that will affect the way people think and feel for a generation or more? My feeling is that it's big and it's going to be with us for a long time.

Ever since the end of World War II, the baby-boomer generation, the Trente Glorieuses, the collapse of Communism and the End of History, all societies more or less everywhere have been brought up to believe that our purpose – our core aim in life – is to get richer and to enjoy it. 'Consumerism' is the word we use. This generation is richer than the last; the next generation should be richer than ours and healthier – only maybe it won't be. All societies, all nations, are judged in terms of GDP: 'How far up the wealth ladder is our country?' Of course, education, health and other factors are taken into account, but it's how rich you are and how fast you can get richer that has really mattered. A good education has been valuable only because you can get a better-paid job at the end of it.

However, over the last few years, this belief – previously hardly challenged; accepted more or less unquestioningly – has been gradually undermined and eroded. Have we been destroying ourselves and the planet we live on by trying to grab too much for ourselves ... now?

Global warming, sustainability, the environment, too many people, too much inequality, even religious fundamentalism are all manifestations of unease about the way we live now. None of this has happened suddenly. A change of mood has gradually been creeping up on us. And that, I think, is where authenticity is coming from.

If I am right and we are seeing the beginnings of a fundamental change of mood, it will profoundly affect corporations and their brands as much as consumers. In fact, it already has. The whole issue of corporate social responsibility, of what the corporation can contribute to society, of who the corporation's stakeholders are: all this is some kind of reflection of authenticity. Put another way, it's about: how authentic is the corporation?

Many of the world's greatest organizations were built on clear values. It may seem strange to read this now but companies like Barclays – which has until very recently been in hot competition for the ultimate untrustworthy brand – were built by Quaker families, whose catchwords were trust and loyalty: no lying to or cheating their customers, no exploitation of their workforce. The confectionery manufacturers Rowntree and Cadbury in the UK, the eccentric, virtually loony Henry Ford in the US, Jamshedji Tata in India: all built companies based around trust. 'If we make it or if we deal with you, you can trust us. We are authentic. We stand behind it. We don't need to write pompous, repetitive, empty mission and vision statements. We don't need to talk about our values. Everyone can see them over generations.'

Sadly, for many of these companies and their competitors, all that has been thrown away. This is why a new generation of companies is emerging with the old values projected in a way that 21st-century customers can understand and, maybe, believe in.

An interesting example of this newer breed of company, which implies authentic without quite saying so, is Richard Branson's Virgin. Everybody who has heard of Virgin knows that it stands for being breezy, cheerful, informal and knocking the fat cats. Virgin is the alternative. Virgin does things a bit differently. And whatever Virgin does is recognizably Virgin.

At the very least, the company is unusual. It had the guts to challenge Britain's Department of Transport in the law courts when it lost a bid to renew a rail franchise ... and the Department backed down. It takes something special to do that. So is Virgin about authenticity, and can you trust it? Well, sort of. Although Branson's move to Necker, his tax-free Caribbean island, for 'health reasons', doesn't necessarily help the Virgin brand.

• • •

In this chapter I've focused largely on product brands – food, drink and clothes. If you source the product carefully and you market it effectively, you create an atmosphere of authenticity.

But brands are not only about fast moving consumer goods; they can be about a whole experience which may last years. Buying a car is one thing; getting it serviced year after year is another, rather different and mostly worse experience. We relate to individuals from a corporation, say an airline or a bank or a mobile phone service provider, through a series of different experiences over a long period of time. Most of these experiences are bad. There's rarely real continuity and there's a lot of mindless bureaucracy. That is the real test for authenticity inside the corporation.

Does the corporation behave consistently, whoever we deal with? Do we actually know what to expect from it? Does it practise what it preaches? Is it a brand we can trust in all kinds of circumstances? Does it apologize when things go wrong? Can we really believe what it tells us, or do we have to look very carefully at the small print? Much too frequently the answer is no ... and we look at some of the reasons why in the next chapter.

2

Corporate Confusion.

In 1925, Bruce Barton, one of the founders of the global advertising agency BBDO, wrote a novel called *The Man Nobody Knows*, which portrayed Jesus Christ as a successful businessman. If Christ were alive in the 1920s, Barton's book imagines, he would be an advertising man. This was, of course, a time in American history when successful businessmen were hero figures. *The Machine Age in America: 1918–1941* has it just about right: *'In the 1920s under three Republican presidents, Harding, Coolidge and Hoover, business never ranked higher [in American esteem].'*[1]

Fat chance of that happening now. The world says it doesn't love big business anymore. It's virtually impossible to switch on television, read a newspaper or look online without seeing flagrant examples of corporate misbehaviour. Just, for example, because they are high profile, look at multinational companies like Starbucks, Amazon and Google, who owe no allegiance to any nation and pay as little tax anywhere as they can get away with through the exploitation of legal and fiscal loopholes, all abetted by multinational legal and accounting firms. After a public outcry in 2012, Starbucks UK said it had decided to pay a bit of tax after all. The British public, quite reasonably, appeared to take the view that it was not up to Starbucks to decide how much to pay to Her Majesty's Revenue and Customs.

Then there are the energy companies, electricity and gas, all engaged in a cartel to raise retail prices and cheat consumers. And the banks – in fact, the whole financial sector. Not just 'casino' banking, taking massive and uncontrolled risks with other people's money through deals so arcane, devious and risky that many of the individuals involved did not themselves understand what they were doing, but also in the 'respectable' side of the business, being complicit in hiding assets stolen from who knows whom, who knows when, on behalf of drug dealers, politicians from pariah regimes and other villainous creatures and organizations. And then deliberately selling inappropriate products to customers and swindling them out of their earnings and savings. Virtually every major bank, especially and sadly in Britain, appears to have been involved, meddling profitably in one piece of dirt after another.

Perhaps the worst characteristic of these organizations is that they say so many different things, at the same time, to so many different audiences, that in the end nobody can really believe a word they say, including their own people. The global public relations company Edelman, in a survey quoted by *The Economist*, found that *'only 18% of people trust business leaders to tell the truth'*.[2] As many as that!

Worst of all their sins is breaking trust with customers. Contradictions flourish and double-think and double-speak rule, as trust between customer and corporation breaks down. Most people can forgive the odd mistake: everybody makes mistakes and does things wrong; we are all a bit inefficient and incompetent sometimes; and when we apologize properly, it usually improves the relationship. But what none of us can forgive is deliberate, premeditated deceit. Once trust is lost between individuals or between individuals and the corporation, it's gone forever.

But many corporations deceive their clients as a matter of course: obscure details in the small print, price rises without warning, and, quite often, deliberate deception of current loyal customers. Let's look at a petty but, to my mind, potent example of deliberate deceit – from a financial institution, of course.

ING Direct, the UK online retail bank, was a small subsidiary of the giant Dutch banking group ING and is now owned by Barclays, itself an organization making heroic efforts to regain trust. ING Direct promoted itself as 'the Decent Bank'. I was a long-time customer and I thought I knew what the company was like – boring, predictable and honest. I trusted it. Then I discovered, quite by chance, that it was offering considerably higher interest rates on deposits to new customers than to people like me, who had been with the organization for years. So I wrote to the CEO asking for an explanation. He didn't personally trouble himself to reply but one of his underlings

did and, with some elaboration, refused on the basis that I was
not a new customer but, if I left and came back six months later,
I would get the new rate. Not only was there not the slightest
suggestion of an apology but there was not even a hint of
embarrassment. For me, this act of petty betrayal left a very
nasty taste. I felt deceived and insulted. I will never go near
ING in any of its manifestations again. Is this an over-reaction?
Maybe but, if it is, it's not unusual.

Fundamentally, the ING example is about contempt for,
and exploitation of, loyalty. *'Rewards are offered increasingly to
the disloyal. Loyalty and, therefore, trust are punished,'* says Brian
Brooks, author of a report on the subject quoted by Anne Karpf
in *The Guardian* newspaper.[3] She also quotes a piece from *Time*
magazine: *'We appreciate your business and as thanks for being a loyal
customer all these years we're going to overcharge you.'*

The sad truth is that – because of this endless exposure of
deceit in so much corporate behaviour – the public mood is,
hardly surprisingly, growing more cynical. Put simply, the world
is losing trust in business. We just do not believe what they tell
us anymore. Big business isn't innocent until proven guilty; it's
the other way round. Of course, this isn't true of all companies
everywhere in the world. Plenty of corporations behave well, at
least most of the time, but they seem to be heavily outnumbered.

Although many people in Western countries have always
been a bit suspicious of the capitalist ethos and there has
always been hostility to it, the alternative has generally appeared
to be much worse – equally corrupt but viciously authoritarian
as well. But the public climate surrounding the corporation
has changed for three major reasons. These are interlinked and
mutually reinforcing.

The first reason is more exposure, leading to more scrutiny and more scepticism. Because of the internet and its various offspring, every individual and every company is more open to scrutiny than ever before. We all feel we have the right to know everything. Detailed scrutiny almost inevitably leads to greater scepticism.

The second reason is that the world in which the multinational operates is increasingly complex, inward-looking and fragmented. Everything is complicated: sourcing, manufacturing, supply chain; even marketing, purportedly driven by the customer, is increasingly about process and quantification. The company talks less and less to the outside world, and its different bits don't talk to each other. As the organization becomes increasingly obsessed with itself, it forgets about its customers, who are often treated as though they are an irritating nuisance, or as material to be plundered, or both.

The third and possibly most significant reason is the ambivalent and partial way in which organizations are attempting to deal with sustainability, global warming, environmental management and the rest of it – in other words, the current zeitgeist. All these issues struggle in the corporate psyche against the fundamental and raw spirit of the capitalist ethos: make as much as you can, get as big as you can, beat the competition any way that you can and focus on winning, however you do it.

It's these three factors – scrutiny and scepticism, internal fragmentation and the changing spirit of the times – that are having a profound and, for the most part, unfortunate impact on the way the corporation behaves and is perceived.

1. Scrutiny and Scepticism

Historically, business has not had a particularly good press. Bruce Barton in the 1920s was a bit of an exception. In the 19th century Balzac, Dickens and Trollope were all scathing. In *The Way We Live Now*, Melmotte, Trollope's swindling hero/villain, could be a creature straight out of a 21st-century novel by Justin Cartwright or John Lanchester. In the United States, Upton Sinclair at the turn of the 20th century was called a 'muckraker' because of his anti-business novels.

In the last few years, though, the attacks on business behaviour have become more frequent and ferocious. Since the turn of the century there has been a cascade of novels, films, documentaries and other stuff on the financial industry, and banking in particular: for example, *Whoops!* by John Lanchester (2010); *Money Never Sleeps* (2010), Oliver Stone's sequel to his earlier success *Wall Street* (1987); and, of course, Michael Moore's *Capitalism: A Love Story* (2009). There have also been well-researched, extremely detailed critiques of the fast food industry (*Fast Food Nation: The Dark Side of the All-American Meal* by Eric Schlosser, 2002), the pharmaceutical world (*Bad Pharma: How Drug Companies Mislead Doctors and Harm Patients* by Ben Goldacre, 2012), the oil industry (*Crude World: The Violent Twilight of Oil* by Peter Maass, 2009) and even my own little world of branding (*No Logo* by Naomi Klein, 1999).

Even the most inquisitive and tyrannical totalitarian government in the second half of the 20th century – even the rulers of the German Democratic Republic in its heyday, making the fullest possible use of all its Stasi informants – knew less about the habits of its citizens than a well-informed retail business does about its customers today. Nowadays, companies

He had indeed conversed so entirely with money, that it may be almost doubted whether he imagined there was any other thing really existing in the world; this at least may be certainly averred, that he firmly believed nothing else to have any real value.

From Tom Jones, *the novel by Henry Fielding, 1749.*

have so much information about virtually all of the habits of their customers that they hardly know what to do with it all.

If a corporation chooses to, it can find out through Google, Amazon and so on what we habitually buy, where we buy it, what we look at when we shop, what we spend, how we buy online, whether our eating habits are consistent, how we spend our leisure time – practically everything about us.

The company can anticipate all our needs and our wants. At least it thinks it can. And, using the same tools and the same networks, we consumers can learn almost as much about the company. We can easily penetrate the corporation behind its brands to find out who directs it. Greenpeace, Amnesty International and others like them can expose a corporation's allegedly ruthless behaviour towards the environment, endangered species, local people and global warming – and regularly do. We can even find out how big corporations dodge taxes; how they sometimes collude with governments to reduce their tax 'burden'. We can learn how obscene are the sums that some bankers earn.

There has never ever been anything like this mutual exposure. There's just no point in hiding anymore. We can look at how the corporation behaves or, at least, how it says it behaves to its various stakeholders; we can find out just about everything. That is why, of course, increasingly, large consumer goods companies, like Unilever, Nestlé and P&G, are endorsing their brands with their corporate name.

And then we can hit back. Or at least we can try to. We can use a Facebook page to tell a company exactly what we think of its behaviour. We can, very occasionally, praise it or, more often, savage it. We can make our feelings very clear … and we do. When

"At UBS we promote a corporate culture that adheres to the highest ethical standards across all areas of our business. Our commitment to excellence in all we do, combined with a desire to understand and fulfil our clients' requirements translates into our client dining experience. That is why, where possible, our menus are crafted from the finest seasonal produce which is ethically sourced, organic and unsurpassed in quality and value. **Just like our business.**"

UBS fined $1.5bn over Libor fix as the watchdogs clamp down.

US seeks to extradite former trader from UK for 'conspiring to manipulate the key rate'

a big energy company, a Shell or a BP or an Eon, does something we don't like, we can relatively easily mobilize a mass movement online. We have certainly let the big banks know what we think of them, not that they have taken much notice. Some NGOs and charities are particularly good at giving corporations of whom they disapprove a bad time: for example, ILRF (International Labor Rights Forum), an anti-sweatshop NGO based in the United States, has been very active in petitioning for increased safety in the workplace in Bangladesh and elsewhere. All of this should help corporations and their customers understand each other a lot better. But, for the most part, it doesn't.

Paradoxically, as corporations learn more about us and we learn more about them, we seem to have less and less personal

Lucy Kellaway of The Financial Times *quotes from a UBS luncheon menu (top); a headline a bit later (above).*

contact. We deal with them, whoever they are, increasingly remotely, so although at one level we are more familiar with each other, at another we are more distant – because we don't actually talk to each other. There's virtually no personal, social exchange.

Does anybody visit their bank manager anymore? We don't have bank managers now; we have 'relationship managers' instead. That name alone should tell us something. Relate is the NGO you go to when your personal relationships are breaking down. Although many of us are, in my judgment, quite rightly, very critical of many large corporations, we don't in real life interact very much with the people inside them. We are out of touch with them because they are out of touch with us. We don't talk to them and they don't talk to us. Perhaps that's why so much advertising from big corporations is so ludicrous that it bears no relationship to what any customer in their right mind actually thinks or feels about it.

The proportion of individuals within the United States who transferred their business from one bank to another in 2011 was 8.7%. The proportion of people in the United Kingdom who said in 2013 that they didn't trust their bank was 43%. There really is a breakdown of trust – and not only with banks.

So does this mean that corporations with big brands can ignore customers and just do what they feel like? No, it doesn't, because the internet and social media have made it much easier for small companies to emerge, for individuals to find a space to launch their own brands, and for innovative and creative people to create a brand that gets an audience, makes a new market and sometimes becomes very successful. It's probably easier to launch a small new company based around an original thought, idea or product today than it ever has been.

In reality, the first few decades of the 21st century will be a very confusing time. Big companies are becoming bigger, more powerful, more global, ignoring national boundaries and national affiliations, getting investment from all over the world, doing a lot of talking and pretending that they are listening, many of them behaving quite as selfishly and greedily as they did before anybody really knew what they were up to – and, simultaneously, they are exposed to public opinion more than ever. And yet, curiously, there has never been a time when there were so many entrepreneurial possibilities for individuals and where small companies with big ideas have had so many great opportunities.

There was never, I believe, a period in the whole of my lifetime when raw nastiness and greed in business, which must always have existed, have been more publicly exposed. Is this because business behaviour has actually got worse, or do we simply hear more about it? My own view is that business behaviour has not changed much; it's just that there's a lot more informed scrutiny.

2. Fragmentation

Business faces a storm of criticism at a time when it's becoming much more complex, self-obsessed and, despite all the chatter about marketing and the consumer, inward-looking.

There's the problem of absorbing acquisitions that are alien in culture and product. How do businesses assimilate the companies and brands they acquire so that they fit comfortably into the whole without losing the characteristics for which they were bought in the first place? If the acquiring corporation has a different national and cultural background from the business it's taking over, does it take a hands-off approach (like Tata has with Jaguar and Land Rover), or does it go right in there and turn it into part of itself (like Santander and Abbey, or Quaker and Snapple), in which case, it may be in danger of overwhelming and then destroying the very thing it has just bought. There's nothing new about this dilemma, but it's getting harder to deal with: first, because the Western cultural pattern no longer dominates in the way it once did, and, second, because increasingly there's a demand for products that, as I pointed out in Chapter 1, are both authentic and local.

This brings us to the issue of adaptation. How far do you adapt what you do so that your products appear to fit local cultural patterns? McDonald's must have a few difficulties here. Presenting what is, after all, a business making and selling chunks of meat stuck on bread to a nation whose population is largely vegetarian, like India, must be a bit of a conundrum. Somehow or other McDonald's seems to manage it ... just. In France, no doubt as a nod towards French individualism, the company serves a single shot of espresso accompanied by three delicate pastries, including a tiny macaroon (this delight is called 'Le Café Gourmand'). Other multinationals face similar problems. In China, Starbucks sells a special line of teas – Mudan white tea, Jinxuan Oolong and Biluochun green tea – in addition to the classics like Earl Grey and English Breakfast. Now those are gestures!

Then there's the supply chain, with everything being sourced through a complex mesh with umpteen intermediaries. Who controls it and how?

All this, of course, impacts on the basis of matrix management. How far do you permit each national management to operate separately? That's a whole world of argument about territorial behaviour and historical cultural patterns.

Next there are silos. All large organizations divide themselves, so far as they can, into separate fiefdoms, which are highly political and carefully guarded. What happens when there's an overlap in functions? Like, for instance, in what's called 'brand engagement', that is, internal marketing; marketing your own corporation's brand strategy to your own employees. Although HR traditionally looks after the corporation's own employees (that's why it's called Human Resources), the marketing and branding people traditionally look after the brand, which is the way things grew up when marketing was an external function only. But now, since the brand operates both internally and externally, which of the two units, HR or marketing, is in charge? Or is it neither? Or are both?

Operationally, if they remain uncontrolled, these silos can destroy a business. If you think this is an exaggeration, there's Sony. Just look at this from the *FT Magazine*:[4]

'Why No One's Listening to a Walkman

'[As] Sony swelled in size and moved into endless new fields (including media), a silo mentality set in. Most notably, each separate department became increasingly determined to protect its own success, as a mini-fiefdom, reluctant to share its ideas in a creative manner.

'The Walkman was a case in point. By the 1990s, it was clear to Sony executives that its successor would be a mobile digital music device. Sony seemed brilliantly placed to develop this since it had a music division and consumer electronics department. But the different departments would not collaborate; on the contrary, there was such rivalry that in 1999, at a consumer electronics fair, they actually launched competing products.

*These cannibalised each other – and created space for Apple to launch the
iPod, which soon swept the market....*

*'[When Sir Howard Stringer, Sony's former CEO,] tried to launch an
"ebook" reader – long before Amazon developed the Kindle device – he
faced resistance because Sony staff did not understand the advantage of
producing revenues for two, not one, departments.'*

As my colleague Daren Cook has pointed out, on top of
all that, when Sony produced a successor to the Walkman, a
particularly brilliant brand name, they called it the Discman,
thereby missing the point completely!

In my experience, Sony's problems are not untypical.
There's confusion at the top, internecine war and therefore lost
opportunities everywhere else in the company, and that's how
things go wrong.

Another example is insurance. There's the large blank
wall between the sales people, who are heavily incentivized
to sell products to customers even when those products are
inappropriate, and the claims people who assume that all
claimants (that is, customers, of course) are liars – and more
or less, as a matter of principle, dispute any claim when there's
the slightest chance that they will get away with it. So if your
daughter has an accident while vacationing in Thailand, you
have to prove she didn't do it on purpose and wait for a few
months before they graciously decide to pay for her to come
home ... or maybe not.

All this is part of the quotidian life of the major corporation
and it exacerbates lack of clarity, and it inevitably leads to a focus
on internal political point-scoring rather than on the outside
world. So who suffers? Why, we the customers do.

Even when the multinational organization recognizes the world beyond itself, it is tempted to build an internal universe to deal with outsiders remotely, through websites, through emails, through blogs and tweets, which avoid personal contact and personal relationships. Despite all the marketing and branding hype, relationships between most service providers and their publics are getting more rather than less distant. Look at the internet to see how many customers are fed up with the way they are treated.

And it gets worse. More and more activities are being outsourced, from office cleaning to tax fixing, which leads to outsiders, who know virtually nothing about the corporation, representing it to its customers. If, as a customer, your only personal relationship with the people you buy from is the UPS delivery man and he, unlike the postman, changes every time there's a delivery, there's not likely to be much mutual warmth.

These mistakes are made as much in new exciting businesses, driven by tech-savvy, marketing-savvy young people as in traditional corporations. They deal with their customers remotely, which means they can almost forget the world outside. Here's what my colleague in Saffron, Ian Stephens, told me of the launch of the new 4G service from EE in the UK in 2012:[5]

'I've been an Orange customer for fifteen years. When EE launched, I transferred across to EE to get the new 4G service. The operator talked as if I was changing networks – "Leaving Orange" – even though I knew they were the same company. Since then I've encountered lots of small but ultimately frustrating glitches caused by the complexity of the system and processes.

1. *I've disappeared from the Orange online and automated telephone system (even though I owe them money and wanted to pay a bill) because their system now seems to regard me as a "lost customer".*

2. *I get texts from both EE and Orange on the same day telling me contradictory things – "pay this now", "don't pay this now because we made an error", two paper bills for November (one from Orange, the other from EE) – neither seeming to acknowledge the other's existence.*

3. *If you try and speak to a human operator to try and sort it out you get a message saying: "Orange/EE is dedicated to excellent customer service…. We are experiencing a very high number of calls. Your call will be answered in 1 hour and 10 minutes." I've tried this several times and whatever time of day it is they always seem to be "experiencing a very high number of calls".*

4. *One trick I've learned is that the fastest way to get a human to answer is to select the button they read out that says "Press X if you are thinking of leaving Orange". They usually answer that one pretty promptly, funnily enough.'*

So EE, the new exciting 4G operator, seems to be just another organization obsessed with its own processes and operations. This incident isn't just another chunk of anecdotal evidence; it's the norm. And everyone, everywhere, is fed up with it.

So much, then, for the first two major threats facing the corporation. But another difficult and complex threat is the corporation's own ambivalence about who it is and what it's there for – its shareholders, its customers, its own management (that is, itself) or the world at large.

3. The Changing Spirit of the Times

Corporate social responsibility (CSR) – the third issue, in the broadest sense – is the biggest problem of all. There's an intense pressure on the corporation to have a wider remit. That's why virtually every major organization, everywhere in the world, claims to have a sense of social responsibility.

Of course, many of the people who run large corporates want to behave well, not only because they feel it's right, but also because they feel it will help the corporation. If being a good company means being admired, this, they believe, will have longer-term benefits in terms of reputation and, therefore, of recruitment, share price, opportunities for acquisition, moves into new territories, and so on.

So, if demonstrating a sense of CSR is good for the reputation of the company, as well as being a good thing to do for its own sake, then they will go ahead and try to do it ... until things get too complicated, or there's some issue that's more immediately pressing. But how does CSR affect the efficient functioning of the business, and where does it begin and end? Sometimes CSR can be a very complex and involved issue and it can therefore mean that companies get out of their depth ... fast.

Just take one simple example: sourcing. Major retailers and manufacturers worldwide are continually being accused of exploiting child labour in their suppliers' plants. If things are to change and High Street retailers are truly going to be held responsible for the behaviour of their suppliers, then traditional ideas around purchasing have to be modified. That is agreed – at least in principle.

So what does it imply? Let's just say we are a major women's clothing retailer. We franchise hundreds of stores in different countries. We focus on fast, constantly changing, inexpensive fashion. Our stores look good, with a strong, consistent, visual identity, and our staff are trained to help customers unobtrusively. Since our clothes are both cheap and always changing, we inevitably rely on a complex supply chain. Our purchasing people look for price, quality, flexibility and reliable delivery. They are trained to believe that our suppliers, who, of course, are based largely in emerging markets, are part of our corporate family: 'We have standards of good behaviour to sustain. We must not be accused of exploiting child labour; on the contrary, part of our corporate philosophy is to raise living standards wherever we go.'

How do sourcing people handle this? Even if they get a lot of help from specialists, experts in the culture and social patterns of the societies with which they work, sourcing staff are genuinely going to find it difficult to fully comprehend what's expected of them. They can't really judge whether the suppliers they deal with behave properly to their own employees according to their own cultural norms. They are out of their depth, and so is the corporation they work for.

This raises huge issues for the organization as a whole. Is it really there, at least in part, to help raise education and health standards among its suppliers in emerging markets? Or, putting it another way, is it there to poke its nose into the way the Vietnamese or the Bangladeshis bring up their children? Is that the way it should handle CSR?

Well, in a world where scrutiny and scepticism are paramount, apparently it is. Over the last few years many of the world's greatest brands – Nike and Gap, among them – have been 'named and shamed'. On 1 June 2012 Anti-Slavery International launched a report called 'Slavery on the High Street' in which over a dozen major Western clothing retailers, 'including high-street stores, Marks & Spencer, Mothercare and the supermarket, Tesco, were accused of selling clothing made by girls in slavery in southern India'. The report is detailed and shocking, but hardly a surprise.

The sad truth is that true CSR isn't always a comfortable fit. If a corporation is genuinely going to be socially responsible, this demands a consistent, long-term attitude that will sometimes take it into unfamiliar, unprofitable and uncomfortable areas of activity. It's a real dilemma. The debate has hardly seriously begun, and its implications are vast.

It means introducing into, and imposing on, an organization a single cultural idea which may be alien to different parts of the business. It can mean major internal conflict, leading ultimately to discussion, to argument and compromise, or to disaster. It can derive from relatively minor acts of short-sighted greed, or it can be much worse. It can even become a horror story. And that is what happened at BP.

• • •

The BP saga is, of course, the classic, but the whole sad tale bears repetition because it illustrates so dramatically the errors that are made by organizations which don't think through the implications of driving potentially conflicting policies and cultures simultaneously.

During the reign of the hyperactive and brilliant John Browne as CEO (1995–2007), BP, sensing the mood of the times, proclaimed that it would look 'Beyond Petroleum' for sources of global energy. In a stroke, the company positioned itself as the global oil industry's leader in the search for sustainability and for solutions to environmental degradation, for which it was so frequently savaged. BP saw how the zeitgeist was changing and seized the moment. As a dramatic part of this process, it launched a new visual identity. It changed its outward and visible manifestations from dreary and neo-military to bold and aspirational. All this was no doubt genuinely felt by the company's leaders: there's no reason to doubt their integrity. But it also seemed to be a shrewd move. A huge company, one of the world's biggest, in an industry highly sensitive to charges of bad environmental behaviour, showing the way forward: such a move would help recruitment, engage public sympathy, keep the corporation leading the competition in the race to find new sources of supply, and so on. BP had found a real differentiator, particularly compared with some of its competitors who were thought to be crass and uncaring. So, as some people might put it, BP rebranded itself.

At the same time, BP was growing fast and was extremely ambitious to be the world's No. 1 oil company both in size and profitability, so there was an intense pressure for greater volume and lower costs. This pressure on profitability came from the same place as 'Beyond Petroleum' – the top. For many managers, particularly those in the field, Beyond Petroleum was just a slogan, not much to do with them, and there was nothing they could do about it sitting in Mozambique or Malaysia. But increasing volume and cutting costs was something they could do. It would be seen; they would be rewarded for it.

In retrospect, then, it's clear that there was a profound mismatch between these two drivers of the organization –

one a wish, maybe a dream, to find new sources of energy, and the other mandatory, to cut costs, increase volume: do it, and do it now. So, as managers cut costs, some inevitably went too far. There were some disasters: there were explosions; people were killed. The Texas City Refinery catastrophe in 2005 was appalling. Fifteen people died and 170 were injured. The company was deeply embarrassed. It cost a lot in money and reputation.

But that was relatively minor compared with what happened next. On 20 April 2010, there was a huge explosion on an oil rig off the coast of Louisiana in the United States. The sea-bed explosion on the Deepwater Horizon killed eleven men working on the platform and injured seventeen others. Over months, about five million barrels of crude oil were spilled into the Gulf of Mexico, threatening the world's most valuable fishing industry, miles of tourist beaches, and wetlands and estuaries filled with unique and irreplaceable wildlife, before, on 15 July 2010, it was effectively capped.

At the time this was thought to be the worst oil spillage disaster within living memory. BP was vilified in the media, especially in the US. The company, it was claimed, was a disingenuous humbug – a foreign company, a classically hypocritical British company, operating with double standards, 'destroying our coastline, polluting our waters, ruining the lives and the livelihoods of our folks in the Gulf, at the same time as it proclaims itself the pioneer oil company in global sustainability'. BP paid in dollars for its mistakes. It set up a $20 billion Spill Response Fund and is, as I write this in 2013, continuing to pay many billions of dollars in compensation and damages to more or less anybody who makes a claim, many of whom were in no way affected by the spill. In November 2012, BP agreed to pay $4.5 billion to resolve criminal charges but it still faces civil claims from the US government. And everybody involved, the contractors and the sub-contractors and, of course, BP itself, blames everybody else. Nevertheless, it was BP's reputation, and not the contractors', that was shattered.

In the event, as we now know, the damage was far less than anticipated and the only thing that seems to have suffered in the longer term is the reputation of BP itself. Birdlife has not been destroyed; the local fishing fleets are back at work. Many people in the affected area are now much richer than they ever dreamed of – thanks to BP. Even now, as I write this, BP is on the US government's black list as a company that 'lacks integrity'.

Without being too judgmental, it's clear that this was a disaster of every conceivable kind for BP. The company managed to get each of the three issues discussed earlier in this chapter completely wrong. First, it was not prepared for, or expecting, the public scrutiny it received. Its communications were almost unbelievably incompetent and disastrous. Even now BP has not really made it clear publicly that the predictions of the greatest ecological marine disaster in history were wildly exaggerated. Second, it evidently failed to manage its suppliers and partners properly: BP and its contractors and sub-contractors are still fighting each other. Fragmentation triumphed. And third, and most important, the CSR element was not, truly and deeply, part of the corporate ethos.

• • •

What this story really underlines is that, if you want to be a good global citizen, you have to think it through. You can't talk about going 'Beyond Petroleum', with all its implications of sustainability, environmental protection and so on, on the one hand, and then create an internal atmosphere in which your people take gigantic risks to push up volume and cut costs on the other.

The policy of an organization, any organization, has to be coherent, and, if you genuinely want to be seen to be socially responsible, this may imply that you do not try to maximize profitability at every opportunity in the short term. You have to have a longer-term view. But many organizations find it very difficult to resist temptation. So the lesson is: if you can't resist it, don't pretend.

As we have seen throughout this chapter, it's a difficult world for corporations. The increasing scrutiny and scepticism of the world they live in, their own self-obsession and consequent isolation in operations and process, the increasing pressure to behave responsibly, all mixed up with the visceral, internal demand for success at whatever cost, mean that they are increasingly unclear about who they are and what they are there for. They don't have a clear brand; they have a bit of a mess.

So how do corporations resolve this dilemma? Not easily. We look at some more examples of corporate responses to the 21st-century challenges in the next chapter. But clear answers? Not often. Not yet.

3

Dealing with the New Zeitgeist.

There is a website called 'I Hate Ryanair – The World's Most Hated Airline'. Some marvellous stories have been posted on it. Here's one: *'Ryanair, The World's Most Hated Airline, kept passengers on board a plane for two hours in temperatures of 38 degrees, due to a delay, and the airline not activating cooling systems'*. Here's another: *'Ryanair flight infested with ticks – passengers charged bite fee'*. And another: *'Ryanair emergency descent forced by maintenance errors'*.

The website enthusiastically reports one ghastly incident after another. But this kind of stuff isn't new to Ryanair. On the contrary, it's grist to its mill. The company thrives on notoriety. It exploits public scrutiny – blogs, tweets, social media – for its own promotion. No airline gets more attention. It is an integral ingredient of the Ryanair brand.

The CEO, Michael O'Leary, seems to revel in a reputation for being loud-mouthed and publicity-hungry. It's sometimes difficult to know quite how serious his proposals really are. What's certain is that they get lots of (free) coverage. In 2009, Ryanair announced that it was considering charging £1 to every passenger who wanted to use the toilet. Then it dropped the idea. Surprise, surprise. This ploy must have been worth millions in free publicity. In 2012, O'Leary made another, equally unorthodox proposal: take away seats from the back of the plane and let passengers stand.

O'Leary's personality, with all its posturing, is inextricably linked to Ryanair's overall style. The airline's visual identity is a clumsy joke; its advertising is risibly crude; its staff, although occasionally, perhaps almost accidentally, pleasant, are quite frequently brusque and unsmiling; the uniforms (which they have to pay for) look as though they are made of paper and are embarrassingly ill-fitting. Put another way, the visual manifestations of the identity are all of a piece. And they are an authentic representation of the brand.

Ryanair is unlike any other airline, even its low-price competitors. Its philosophy seems to be very simple: we are very efficient and we have strict rules; that's why we are so cheap. And just to underline that, everything about us looks cheap. We can offer the lowest fares on any route and, if you obey all our very strict rules, there will be no problem. If you don't, we will charge you as much as we feel like, which will be a lot.

It's quite clear that Ryanair uses every opportunity it can to make money out of its passengers. If there's the slightest infringement of any of its regulations, which, although cumbersome, are quite clearly set out, the airline is utterly ruthless. *'Woman forced to pay £200 to print out Ryanair tickets'* is one small example.[1] Ryanair has no hesitation in stopping people boarding, or even in throwing them off the aircraft, if they can't pay for extras that break the rules.

O'Leary's thinking, when you strip away the rant and the bluster, is that flying short distances isn't about fun or glamour. It's like taking a bus or subway, and it's perfectly safe. In fact, it's by far the safest means of transport. You don't need seat belts any more than you do on a train, so there really is no reason to sit down. If you want to pay less, you should be allowed to stand. You just need an economical, punctual ride.

This is an original and attractive point of view, and in the essentials it appears Ryanair does actually get it mostly right – more right than many of its competitors. It loses fewer bags (0.5 bags per 1,000 passengers, compared with 16 bags per 1,000 on British Airways);[2] it has fewer flight cancellations; and it arrives on time more frequently. Despite its reputation as 'the least liked airline' (TripAdvisor poll),[3] it carries more passengers than any other airline in Europe,[4] and its sales and profits annually increase. So it's clear that detailed public scrutiny works for Ryanair. All the blogs and the tweets and the appalling publicity help Ryanair to grow and grow.

On the issue of corporate social responsibility (CSR), the company's view is also quite straightforward. Ryanair doesn't claim it wants to make the world a better place: it doesn't care if the world is a better place or not. It has never heard of a carbon footprint. It doesn't claim it exists to encourage people to go to places they could otherwise not afford; it doesn't talk about making the world more prosperous by opening up smaller cities to tourism and investment; it doesn't talk about how its flights

*On Ryanair, standing up might
be more comfortable than sitting
down...*

enable people living away from home to get together regularly with their friends and families. It doesn't say that, with Ryanair, what for half a century was a privilege of the very few, is now available to everyone. Ryanair doesn't have a CSR policy. It simply says: 'Give us the money and obey the rules, and we will take you there, cheaply and punctually.' So, not to put too fine a point on it, with Ryanair you know exactly where you are and you know exactly what you're getting. It is a model of clarity and authenticity.

Curiously, as I write this, O'Leary has made some kind of modest gesture which acknowledges that Ryanair's behaviour may have gone too far. He says that Ryanair has to be a bit more thoughtful with its customers. Well, we'll have to see, won't we?

For now, if we look at the three core issues discussed in Chapter 2, it is clear that Ryanair intuitively understands all of them and, in its own way, it deals with them. Public scrutiny? It gets plenty of that and enjoys it. Internal fragmentation? Absolutely not: what the boss says goes, and how Ryanair behaves internally is publicly followed through in the behaviour of its people and in all its visible manifestations. CSR? There isn't any, so it's not a problem.

Ryanair has a clear and coherent personality and identity, embracing its product, environment, communications and behaviour. In many ways, it's a classic example of branding. Ryanair makes no pretence to be anything other than it is. Wherever you touch it, it's the same – and its CEO is the personification of everything the company stands for.

The reason why Ryanair is such an interesting brand is that the organization, consciously or otherwise, has understood some – although not all – of the profound changes that are taking place in the world in which it operates and, in its own idiosyncratic way, it has responded to them. Ryanair is authentic.

• • •

Other organizations, which may appear on the face of it to be much more aware of their brand, much more concerned about their reputation, are in real life much less sure-footed, much more tentative.

The supermarket Tesco is a business that tries to get it right, and quite often fails. The legend of its origins is a bit like a fairy tale. Jack Cohen, a Cockney Jewish ex-World War I serviceman (Tesco is nearly 100 years old), started out with a barrow and the motto 'pile it high – sell it cheap', and that's what Tesco has been doing with a few variations ever since. It became a truly remarkable business, swallowing up many of its competitors, like Victor Value. It ran circles round the much older and better-established Sainsbury's until – under the direction of one hard-headed, clear-minded, tough guy after another (up to and including Sir Terry Leahy, also like Jack Cohen from a humble background but this time Liverpool Catholic) – it became the UK's acknowledged top supermarket. According to Deloitte,[5] Tesco is the world's third largest supermarket chain, operating in fourteen countries and with a powerful position in many of them (its only significant failure has been in the United States but that's always difficult for foreign companies).

For all its success, however, it's a brand that many people seem not to like much. In the UK, its home market, it's the No. 1 supermarket chain by a long way,[6] but nobody loves it because the myth is that it destroys small traders and the local economy. It makes small towns and city streets look and feel the same. It turns everything into a faceless commodity. That's why we were quite amused when demonstrators threw stones at a new proposed Tesco, and when a partly built store fell onto a railway track in the middle of London's commuter belt.

But what happens when Tesco comes to town? The story goes that the company selects a site within a town and, through the machinations of its estate department and their various satraps and lackeys, it lays siege to the local authority. Eventually, through a mix of cajolery and threats, Tesco gets the site it wants in the town it wants – a country town in Suffolk, say – and tears the heart out of it. Tesco destroys the local economy: the butchers, the fishmongers, the greengrocers all disappear, consumed by a monstrous, voracious, hideous machine masquerading as a supermarket chain.

So what actually happens? Do Tesco tanks roll up and down the High Street, spraying the local shops with machine gun bullets? Do the local shopkeepers panic and close their doors when they hear the dreaded Tesco name? Are hundreds of bemused and bedraggled town and village dwellers herded into camps by Tesco stormtroopers and marched into the new Tesco supermarket?

None of that happens. What happens is perhaps a bit more mundane. People – that is, you and me – moan about Tesco's arrival but, to coin a phrase, we vote with our feet. We just go in and shop. And shop. And keep on shopping. Why? Because Tesco has more variety than the local shops we say we love so much but always abandon; it's easier to park; and it's very often cheaper. Tesco has more choice for less money. So, gradually, we find ourselves doing 'The Big Shop' there and we salve our conscience by going into the small, local shops for a few special things or when we choose to potter around a bit. 'Oh, isn't it lovely here? Such a pity Tesco is forcing them to close.'

The truth of the matter is that Tesco doesn't kill small traders. We do. And if we genuinely didn't prefer Tesco, then we wouldn't choose to go there.

But, nevertheless, Tesco is deeply unlovable. Although in the rational factors that influence choice – quality, variety and price – it is excellent, its stores lack almost all the emotional factors that we love: warmth, charm, any kind of empathy. Tesco's graphics are hideous. Its fascias are a blot on the landscape. Although the strapline 'Every little helps' is strong and persuasive, much of the advertising is feeble. And everywhere it goes, quite regardless of where it is, Tesco looks the same: there's absolutely no sensitivity to place. Somewhere, right in the back of its mind, it still says: 'pile it high – sell it cheap'.

The company also has a reputation for being utterly ruthless with its suppliers. There was a scandal in 2012 when farmers in the UK dairy industry got together to claim that Tesco's pricing policy was ruining them, and another in 2013 when Tesco and other supermarkets were damaged by a fraud in which traces of horsemeat were found in some cheaper meat products. The claim then was that the supermarkets, by implication led by Tesco, demanded such low prices and the meat supply chain was so complex that fraud was almost inevitable. Put another way, Tesco didn't seem to know where some of its meat was coming from. Internally there was fragmentation. While, on the one hand, there was constant pressure on buyers to get the cheapest regardless of where it came from, on the other Tesco's marketing people were emphasizing the wholesome character of its products to its customers. So do Tesco and its suppliers have a relationship based on mutual trust? Apparently not. Should we, the customers, trust Tesco then? Evidently not entirely.

No wonder people don't like Tesco, given its reputation for destroying local environments on the one hand and bullying suppliers into adulterating their products on the other. We do like its variety and low prices, but we do not like its behaviour or appearance. Nor despite its very public apologies do we trust it and now, perhaps belatedly, Tesco seems to have discovered this.

But, despite all this, the strange thing is that, when you look really closely, Tesco is perhaps rather more thoughtful and better behaved than it appears at first sight. For example, it seems to have a lively, interesting and in many ways well-considered CSR policy.

Sustainability, environmental issues, Alzheimers, reducing the carbon footprint, meals for schoolchildren, cancer research – there's hardly an area that Tesco doesn't, one way or another, contribute to. It has its own CSR activities: it works with and supports NGOs and charities around the world, or, putting it another way, it outsources some of its CSR. It has won awards in China, Hungary, Poland and South Korea as a leader in issues around sustainability and environment. But, strangely for such a high-profile organization, and one that should be so sensitive to public perception, it hardly talks about CSR. You have to look quite hard on its website to find out what it does, and there doesn't appear to be much at all in its stores – at least if there is, I haven't seen it. Why? Does Tesco not make the connection between social responsibility and public perception?

The company is, of course, reacting to new developments in shopping habits. It's moving online very fast, and it's also opening more small outlets in the High Street – Tesco Metro and Tesco Express – so it clearly isn't totally insensitive.

Its behaviour with small businesses isn't quite what it seems either. Although Tesco has a reputation for destroying local enterprises, it has actually made several investments in start-up companies. Harris and Hoole, a small coffee-shop chain, is 49% owned by Tesco. Tesco has also made an investment in Dobbie's, the garden centre business, and in the Euphorium Bakery. Tentatively, Tesco is introducing these into a few of its branches. In 2013, the company also announced that it was buying Giraffe, a UK chain of restaurants primarily aimed at children. Why did Tesco buy it? Because people like eating out! Maybe they do, but it's hard to conceive of two brands less like each other than Tesco and Giraffe. The mix is almost incomprehensible. It's as though what Tesco does in CSR and investing in small businesses is a private, internal matter of no public consequence.

In any issue that involves public scrutiny and creating public goodwill, Tesco seems clumsy and maladroit. Until the horsemeat scandal badly shook it, it didn't seem to see that the public mood was changing. Sure, we want it cheap but that isn't the only thing we want. Tesco, like so many other large companies, completely missed out on the idea of authenticity. So is Giraffe intended to be authentic? Maybe.

What should Tesco do to align itself with the changing mood? Here are some thoughts. Why doesn't Tesco introduce small, local brands and shops into its stores to show that, when Tesco comes to town, it helps the locality thrive and doesn't dismiss and ignore it? Why doesn't it turn parts of some of its stores and car parks into farmers' markets on a regular weekly basis? Looked at from a commercial point of view, that would be headline news, worth millions in advertising and public relations. It would help Tesco to get even more sites. It would also alter the way in which Tesco was perceived by the communities in which it operates. Why doesn't it modulate the design of its fascias and interiors according to local environments and encourage staff to be more active in local community activities? In other words, why doesn't it embrace the communities in which it plays such an important part?

Tesco has the rational factors right but it doesn't seem to have understood that, in a world where public scrutiny is so ubiquitous, it needs to sharpen up its practice and demonstrate that underneath its cold, calculating exterior, it has charm and warmth; that it cares – about customers, suppliers and the community as a whole; that it is authentic. Put quite simply: the spirit of the times has changed and Tesco doesn't seem to have noticed.

Like Ryanair, Tesco was built around a very powerful idea – price and choice. Of course, Tesco revolutionized shopping with its huge out-of-town supermarkets just at the moment when every family had a car. Its timing was perfect. But the model seems to be crumbling a bit. Why is it that the Ryanair model is still working, while Tesco is much more troubled? Because Tesco is much more obtrusive ... and intrusive. If you don't like Ryanair you can avoid it, but you can't avoid Tesco. It's much bigger and it's ubiquitous. And there's absolutely nothing to laugh at. Ryanair regularly makes itself look ridiculous. Tesco isn't ridiculous; it's somehow a bit menacing. Can you really trust Tesco? It may be something to do with the organization's internal culture. Maybe, despite its continual contact with its various publics, its internal behaviour patterns are so institutionalized that it doesn't quite understand what goes on in the outside world any more. It just listens to itself. That happens sometimes with big corporations. Well, Tesco needs to start taking notice or it will learn the hard way, because the brand is tainted. It still has the opportunity to get it right. But will it?

. . .

And what about the carbonated drinks and junk food world, facing an obesity and diabetes epidemic? Can it learn anything from tobacco and cancer? Until the last quarter of the 20th century, everybody, all over the world, smoked all the time – cigarettes, cigars, cigarillos, pipes: it was normal. We still get a shock when we look at movies of the 1950s and onwards. Humphrey Bogart as the detective Philip Marlowe, with a cigarette stuck permanently at the end of his lower right lip, leering mournfully at Veronica Lake or Lauren Bacall. Everyone smoked – at meal times, between courses, in aircraft, trains, buses, cars, even on bicycles. The world moved around in a cloud of cigarette smoke and cigarette brands were national, even global symbols. Every nation had its favourites. Marlboro was the Western cowboy: John Wayne on a pack. And there were many others – Camel, Lucky Strike, Winston, all now nearly forgotten, each with its own social nuance and resonance.

In Britain, we had seedy, weedy little Woodbines, robust macho Players Navy Cut and quite a few posher brands, like Passing Cloud, each of which emphasized some small implication of social and cultural snobbery – typically British. In retrospect there were some great slogans. I still especially like, 'For your throat's sake smoke Craven "A"' and 'Ten minutes to wait and mine's a Minor'. A good friend of mine was fired from an advertising agency when he wrote this line for Baron cigarettes: 'Is your wife Baron? Then you must have a filter tip.'

All the major countries had their own symbols in smoke. The French had Gauloises Disque Bleu, with its idiosyncratic pack and unique aroma. You knew you were in French territory when you sniffed the air. It was an intrinsic part of life. The world was simply unimaginable without tobacco and cigarettes and the smell.

And then, gradually, we learned about cancer; that cigarettes killed. And it all began to change. The tobacco companies, of course, vigorously denied it at first. Then they rigged up phoney evidence to show it had absolutely nothing to do with them. Then they ignored it and hoped it would go away. And, for the last decade or two, the industry has been wriggling around in

The doctor's choice, 1939: 'Craven "A" claims its cigarette is good for you, as it is "Made Specially to Prevent Sore Throats".'

a curious mix of shame and bravado, half acknowledging the problem and half pretending it hasn't happened. They even claim that cigarette packaging, on which they've spent billions, doesn't increase the sale of cigarettes! So why do they do it? Altruism?

Gradually, however, despite fighting a long hard rear-guard battle, the tobacco companies have recognized that, in the long term, the game is up – and they are diversifying. It will take a few more years yet, but it looks as if the end of the tobacco industry is inevitable. And this means massive knock-on effects for farmers, for cities with large tobacco manufacturing sites and for taxation policies all over the globe. It also means that the world is becoming a different place. Of course, there's still plenty of tobacco smoke in Russia, China and a lot of other countries, but the writing is on the wall.

And now we are seeing the whole story played out all over again with fizzy drinks and obesity. The companies involved are huge, their brands are global, the financial stakes are colossal and the change in prospect for people's way of life is extremely demanding.

With the emergence of the new zeitgeist and concerns about sustainability, environment and, of course, health, the issue of obesity has gradually emerged as a major problem. The rich world is getting fatter and fatter. The Americans are the fattest people in the world, closely followed, as usual, by the British. According to *The Guardian*, Britain is 'The Fat Man of Europe': *'Britain's doctors say the obesity crisis is unresolvable and over half of all adults will be seriously overweight by 2050.'*[7] And, as the world wobbles its way to death from diabetes, who do the doctors blame? Why the fizzy drinks and junk food companies, of course.

Once again, a huge global industry is threatened by a massive change in the spirit of the times. The obesity threat in the early 21st century is just as significant as the cancer issue was a couple of generations before it, and the major corporations involved face the same set of problems. Only this time the fast moving consumer goods (FMCG) companies are finding that public scrutiny is itself faster ... and harsher. They all have problems – Nestlé, Pepsi-Cola and the others – but the paradigm is Coke.

• • •

The statistics surrounding the Coca-Cola Corporation and its brand are simply staggering. So-called brand valuation experts always rate it among the world's top 10. In 2012, the brand was worth $7.8 billion, according to Interbrand. Coca-Cola and its competitors in FMCG virtually invented consumer branding, and for at least a hundred years they were the admired model. The Coca-Cola story, or versions of it, is still taught at business schools all over the world. For half a century, if you wanted to know how to create and manage a consumer brand, all you had to do was look at Coke. During World War II Coca-Cola moved around the world with American forces and it became one of the first global FMCG brands. Practically everyone, everywhere, fell in love with it.

Paradoxically, bearing in mind its current dilemma, Coca-Cola was invented – perhaps magicked would be a better word – in the late 19th century by John Pemberton, a pharmacist, in Atlanta, Georgia, as a health tonic ... but that brand idea didn't last long. Over the next hundred years or so Coke transformed itself into the incarnation of fun and joy in a bottle, and then a can. The brand was synonymous with the good life all around the world. Coca-Cola was 'the real thing'. Even water seemed to be some kind of inferior substitute. Coke became ubiquitous.

Public scrutiny? Coke couldn't get enough of it. Coca-Cola gleefully danced its way everywhere and into everything. Even the popular image of Santa Claus – a plump, jolly man with a white beard – emerged from Coca-Cola advertising. *'Life became a little sweeter in 2005 as Coca-Cola arrived,'* said *The Economist* about Coke's launch in Syria, of all places.[8] It seemed that junk food and fizzy drinks, the unique gifts of the United States to the entire world, were invincible. Everybody, more or less everywhere, almost literally lapped up the stuff. Authenticity? Forget it.

And now the world of fizzy drinks is starting to fall apart. Fizzy drinks and junk food make you fat and lead to ill health and early death. Maybe I'm exaggerating, but not much. It must be a huge shock to Coca-Cola's system. How can the incarnation of innocent fun be dangerous? For the first time ever, the company and its competitors are on the defensive. 'Sure, we're all about the enjoyment of life, but don't overdo it now! Drink Coke. But not too much. And remember – have fun!' That is what is beginning to happen.

So what should Coca-Cola and, for that matter, its competitors Pepsi-Cola and the others, do about obesity? They have all known about the problem for years, of course, and they have introduced low-sugar, sugar-free and every other conceivable variation on the original product. They all have expensive, high-profile and, in some cases, thoughtful CSR programmes. They have also, rather belatedly, been diversifying. But now, as public scrutiny is getting harsher, they – like the tobacco industry before them – are flailing around. They have reduced the size of their cans and they have promoted indoor and outdoor exercise. But obesity won't go away. McDonald's, Burger King and the rest of them are equally anxious. They virtually tell us the meal comes from fat-free beef! But it's fizzy drinks that are the prime focus.

Fizzy drinks is a vast business. It employs millions of people directly or indirectly; it supports big economies; and it pays a lot in tax around the world. If the Coca-Cola brand becomes tarnished, it will have a major impact on the corporation behind it. All the major corporations in the field are worried, and they are now beginning to talk. It looks as if they are recognizing that they have a public scrutiny problem as well as a major CSR one. How can you, on the one hand, take CSR seriously if, on the other, your main products are so potentially harmful? Pepsi is now promoting healthy drinks and Coke runs advertising programmes about health. Here is a quote from the BBC News:[9]

'Fizzy-drink giant Coca-Cola has launched an advert addressing obesity for the first time on television

'The ad … follows mounting pressure on the soft drinks industry.

   'New York City is preparing to ban large sugary drinks in restaurants, cinemas and stadiums.

   'Coca-Cola has said the video was not made in response to criticism of the soft drink industry, but is an effort to raise awareness.

'"Damage control"

'"There's an important conversation going on about obesity out there and we want to be a part of the conversation," Stuart Kronauge, general manager of sparkling beverages for Coca-Cola North America, told the Associated Press.

'In the advert, a female narrator says Coca-Cola offers smaller portion sizes, is working to make better-tasting, low-calorie sweeteners and has voluntarily made lower-calorie drinks available at schools.

'The video adds: "All calories count, no matter where they come from."

'It says: "If you eat and drink more calories than you burn off, you'll gain weight."

'Another ad … features activities that add up to burning off the "140 happy calories" in a can of Coke.

'But Mike Jacobson, executive director for the Center for Science in the Public Interest, said that if the company was serious about tackling obesity it would stop fighting a tax on its drinks.'

Here is another quote from Joseph Tripodi, Coca-Cola's marketing chief: 'If you are sitting on your ass all day then have a Diet Coke…. We are easy to demonise as we are the world's largest brand and so people say "you guys are causing all the problems"'.[10] So what we are seeing is the tobacco story all over again.

• • •

Of course, over time there will be a tax on soft drinks. New York City, under Mayor Bloomberg's administration, is already proposing it. And it won't be very long before packaging will be plain, there will be warning signs about the danger of death from diabetes, and a ban on some forms of advertising and promotion. Maybe by, say, 2040 Coke and Pepsi, as brands, will have the same position in society as cigarettes today.

It is already clear that the majors are moving away from sugar as fast as they can and getting into the 'authentic' products they ignored for so long. Literally as I write this, I read that Coca-Cola has bought virtually all of the Innocent drinks business that it didn't have before.

My hunch is that if the mood of the times is towards authenticity, then Coca-Cola and the others are going to try to offer it. They may well move into it in a big way. But it's a bit late. Once again, a huge group of brands belonging to the companies that practically invented the commercial branding business have lost touch with what's going on in the world. Still, better late than never, I suppose. It's inevitable that even the world's biggest companies do what we, the consuming public, want in the end. Isn't that nice!

So now, in the next chapter, let's take a look at some of the things a good brand needs to do to look after itself and stay successful in the first part of the 21st century.

4

What Does the Corporation Stand For?

The lesson of at least two of the examples in the last chapter is that if you want to stay in the same place, you have to keep changing, as Montesquieu, or some other clever person, said.

It is perfectly possible to sustain the core idea – 'price and choice', let's say for Tesco, or 'fun and enjoyment' for Coca-Cola – over generations, provided that you keep adapting your product range, the way you look, the way you talk, how you sell, where you sell and the way you act, to the way the world around you is changing. And the world is changing fast. The world is interested in, and sceptical about, the company. The world is poking its nose in.

On top of that, as the world is changing, so the organization is changing too. As it becomes more successful, gets bigger, gobbles up competitors, suppliers and customers in its home country, goes global, moves into allied fields, changes chief executives and other senior people, there's always the likelihood that somewhere or other the original ideas that drove the company will get lost in the machine. New priorities and new competitors emerge; technology moves on; financial imperatives become overwhelming; and, after a bit, sometimes the organization doesn't know what it's there for anymore. It doesn't really know what it is and it may not know what it's trying to do except, if it's in bad shape, survive, and, if it's in good shape, keep winning. That's just when it needs to stop and think and try to find out, once again, what it really is and then act it out authentically for the whole world to see.

The company is porous: the inside and the outside world continually impact on each other. But let's start with the inside. There has to be a flow of clear and distinct messages, all emanating from or endorsed by top management, which continuously underline what the corporation is there for, how it should behave, how it should communicate. Every part of the organization has to absorb this and act it out. The core of all this – the brand essence – must be simple and clear. Of course, it will have to be elaborated and driven home relentlessly. The creation, launch and maintenance of this core idea has become a standard part of business school and management practice. The rules are so well known that they are almost swamped by and disappear under the detail. It's time, I think, to clarify them, briefly, without the aid of diagrams, arrows, boxes, pyramids and overlapping circles which serve to complicate and mystify. Here they are: just five short points. I am indebted to my good friend, Mohi, for some of the thoughts that follow. We have worked on them together. They are as follows:

1. Knowing who you are
2. Talking, listening and being engaged
3. Showing who you are
4. Embracing everything you do
5. Managing it and making it work

1. Knowing Who You Are

- *Who are you?*
- *Why are you here?*
- *What are you trying to do?*

The people who work in a big organization have a multiplicity of cultural, socio-economic, religious and national affiliations. If they are going to develop a genuine corporate loyalty, what they do, how they do it, why they do it, how it contributes to the strength of the whole has to be clearly set out and interpreted for them in a way they can understand, grasp and commit to. As part of all this they have to absorb what is and what isn't acceptable behaviour. So some key sentences or phrases that encapsulate the whole must become the basis from which everyone understands what's expected of them. These key phrases need regular interpretation, adaptation, modulation and elaboration through anecdotes, stories, videos and other examples that are meaningful, memorable, sometimes funny or dramatic, but always authentic and interesting. The idea also needs constant commitment, affirmation and re-affirmation. If you want to, you can call this 'articulating the core idea through the brand platform', or brand essence – in the broadest sense.

The basis must, of course, involve enshrining who you are, what you stand for and what you are trying to achieve, in a short, pithy sentence or two, or even a word or phrase which can then be interpreted and elaborated for every audience and every situation.

The danger, of course, is that writing a sentence or phrase of this kind – a sort of wish list – can too readily degenerate into banal platitudes, which bear no relationship to the reality, and are more or less identical to the kind of things all the competitors are saying. That's why most mission, vision and value statements are so interchangeably mediocre. You have to say something that's simple and recognizably true and doesn't raise a hollow laugh.

So how does the company get it right? The one thing to remember is that every organization somewhere or other is unique. It may be 90% identical to the competitor in terms of rational factors – price, quality and service – but 10% is different and that's the bit to identify, understand and present; that's the bit which is encapsulated in the core idea, in the brand platform; and that's the bit that has to be emphasized and made attractive in the visual and verbal presentation of the organization to all audiences, all the time. Sometimes it's something the corporation isn't conscious of, sometimes it's so obvious it screams out. And it's unique. For Ryanair, when you get right down to it, what makes it different is brutality – and it shows.

2. Talking, Listening and Being Engaged

- *Who are you talking to?*
- *What are you saying?*
- *Who are you having a dialogue with?*
- *Is it relevant?*
- *Who are you listening to?*
- *And how carefully?*

Any organization that's really sizeable makes an impact on a big audience. Any organization that creates change has to have conversations with the audience upon whom these changes will impact, and that potentially could be a global audience. If it's IBM, it's anyone involved in innovation anywhere in the world. If it's Tesco, it's anyone who cares about their neighbourhood. That is why, one way or another, whether they are aware of it or not, most very big corporations talk to a vast world – at least some of the time. Although most people, in most places, may not be very interested, there will be people everywhere who feel a little empathy for the company and its products, and there will also be plenty of people who dislike it or are even enraged by it, or who like it and hate it simultaneously – 'let's Google it'. Many of these individuals nowadays make their opinions clear by going online.

We currently live in a world of tweets, e-mails, texts and other social media, in which we can all scream at each other all the time and the corporation simply has to take time out to listen. And respond. It is vital for the corporation to join in. Some corporations may hear, many may even listen but, for the most part, they don't yet respond – not sensibly or sensitively.

Listening is, in some ways, even more important than talking, partly because it's harder. Of course, we all know about research and focus groups and discussion panels but, deep down, organizations find it hard to truly understand and react effectively to what they are being told. Most organizations hear what they would like to hear, or they don't hear at all. Big corporations are, for the most part, conservative and defensive.

But a company isn't isolated. It communicates – or, at least, it should. Apart from its wider audience, from which it can't escape, there are, of course, all the standard target audiences, both internal and external: the financial audience, and all the other external organizations with which the corporation deals – suppliers, partners, customers, potential customers, competitors, and so on. So how does the corporation communicate with them?

Broadly speaking, the media the organization uses can be divided into three parts: those it pays for (press, posters, television), those it controls (its own internally managed media, website, blog, and so on), and those over which it has no control (social media). It's now customary to talk of paid, owned and earned media. But, in addition to these – the conventional media – the corporation has all kinds of other relationships with customers, with whom it has a daily series of mundane relationships: for example, people paying bills, people having queries, all the daily interactions of life. The corporation may carry out hundreds of thousands, even millions of these transactions every day. They are the transactions that affect the way their customers think of them. The organization must learn to deal with each of these transactions thoughtfully. It must ask the right questions in the right way. It must answer questions in a way that its own people and its partners can understand.

This should happen at every level, including mundane exchanges about, say, invoices or contract renewals, between, let's say, an energy supplier and a householder about a bill, or a bank and its retail customers about a surcharge on an overdraft. But usually it doesn't. The corporation churns out standard, jargon-ridden, obfuscatory officialese. And the customer becomes increasingly bewildered, frustrated and irritated. All this, while in its press and television ads the corporation proclaims its warm, friendly and informal personality, dedicated to making the customer's life easier.

Why does the corporation do this? Because departments don't talk to each other. Because some advertising is nothing to do with real life. Because the corporation doesn't think clearly. Because 'that's the way we do things and that's the way we've always done them'. And, much too often, when the corporation does talk, it mouths a jumble of unbelievable and repetitive clichés.

How can any of us believe that Vodafone actually set up a 'Customer Delight Index', especially when we have to hang on for forty minutes while we pay them to answer our call?

As I was writing this piece, my mobile phone made a little beep and, quite out of the blue, I received the following text from Vodafone:

Q1 of 4: Based on this experience, how likely would you be to recommend Vodafone, from 10 (definitely would) to 0 (definitely would not)?
Wally: 0

Q2 of 4: Did we resolve your issue on this occasion? Please reply with either Yes or No.
W: There was no issue.

Q3 of 4: How satisfied were you with the adviser who handled your query, from 10 (very satisfied) to 0 (very dissatisfied)?
W: There was no discussion about anything. This is typical Vodafone. You've contacted the wrong person and there's no human contact to correct it.

Thanks. Finally please could you tell us the reasons for your ratings?
W: This is Kafka. Just get some human being to check what I have texted and you might just understand.

*We really appreciate your help. Your feedback will be used to help us
continually improve our service to customers.*
W: You absolutely don't understand at all.

Then, ten minutes later, I got another beep and text – also
completely out of the blue:

*Q1 of 4: Based on this experience, how likely would you be to recommend
Vodafone, from 10 (definitely would) to 0 (definitely would not)?*
W: 0

*Q2 of 4: Did we resolve your issue on this occasion? Please reply with either
Yes or No.*
W: No.

*Q3 of 4: How satisfied were you with the adviser who handled your query,
from 10 (very satisfied) to 0 (very dissatisfied)?*
W: 0

Thanks. Finally please could you tell us the reasons for your ratings?
W: Because you have no empathy. It's all by the book. Inhuman,
unhelpful and absurdly bureaucratic.

*We really appreciate your help. Your feedback will be used to help us
continually improve our service to customers.*
W: That response exemplifies precisely what I'm saying. It's all
mindless button-pushing bureaucracy.

Since then I've heard nothing – nothing at all.

Vodafone are not the only ones; they just happen to be typical. The airwaves and internet are filled up with this mindless, repetitive rubbish.

How many of us so-called customers smile with anticipatory delight when we are told by BA stewards to 'sit back, relax and enjoy the flight'? Nobody believes any of this: not the people who write this stuff, not the people who speak it and not the poor old customers who have to put up with it. Some of the language is bewilderingly comic. 'A warm welcome on board on behalf of myself and that of the captain.' Who, in real life, says that kind of thing?

But it should not be like that. If you're inside the corporation communicating with someone on the outside, just ask yourself: what do you want out of the dialogue or discussion, and what does your respondent want? What has to happen next? Ask yourself how you can stay relevant and clear. And how can what you say and do relate to what other bits of the organization say and do? Remember: you want a result.

3. Showing Who You Are

- *How to look*
- *How to talk*
- *How to show you are you*

What you look like, how you talk and how you behave underlines and emphasizes who you are. We immediately recognize the symbol of the Red Cross, the Stars and Stripes, and the logo of Mercedes-Benz or Apple. Their symbolism is powerful and it reminds us who they are. Behind each symbol lies an idea. If you have a clear, core idea – that is, a clear idea of who you are and what your purpose is; put another way, if you have a clear brand platform – you should be able to visualize it in a way that's unique, compelling and immediately recognizable. It's not just the symbol: everything you do should fit. It should be adaptable to different circumstances and situations and modulated over time so that, however you present yourself and wherever you are seen, in whatever situation, you are you and your audiences recognize you. They recognize what you look like, they recognize how you talk, they recognize your tone of voice and how you behave. In other words, you project a clear personality.

There has been so much written on all of these things by so many communication specialists (including me) that it would be otiose to go through the steps all over again. There are plenty of people to talk to, plenty of consultants to see and plenty of books to read, so what I've just written is an introduction, if you don't know it – and a reminder, if you do.

4. Embracing Everything You Do

- *Product*
- *Environments*
- *Communication*
- *Behaviour*

Some messages aren't conveyed in words. Apple's message, for example – what Apple wants to say about itself – emerges most powerfully and influentially in its products. What you hold in your hand and what you see on a screen reinforces Apple's idea of itself. Its core idea is in its products.

So, to underline a point I've made several times: the brand emerges in your products, in your environments, your offices, your factories, your retail outlets, and in the behaviour of your people, as well as in communications of all kinds. It's what happens when you meet a brand in any of its manifestations. It's what is increasingly being called 'brand experience'. Most organizations still do not make that connection and the ones that do, partly at any rate because of silos and internal fragmentation, forget it – at least some of the time.

5. Managing It and Making It Work

To make all this work – to project a clear personality, identity or brand, if you prefer – the organization needs to be totally committed. And this commitment has to come from the top. If people within the corporation as a whole, and its various different sectors, see that top management understands and devotes time and energy to it, then they will follow. And if the leadership is committed for long enough, then the core idea, what the organization is really about, becomes institutionalized; it becomes part of 'what we do' and 'how we do things', and it gets absorbed into the corporation's bloodstream. But if it's not given long-term commitment, it will simply disintegrate into a form of words, an irrelevance – nothing to do with real life.

Once it's clear that such commitment exists and is sustained – at the top – it has to be managed throughout the company. There has to be one individual or, more probably, a small group, who can align the activities of all departments and divisions so that everyone, everywhere, speaks with one voice. There's a real management and co-ordination issue here. How do you co-ordinate an activity that runs across marketing, HR, recruitment, CSR, product design, properties, sourcing and every other area of the business and that also has global impact? There's no single formula. Each organization has to try to work out its own solution. If there's sufficient long-term commitment, there always will be a solution.

• • •

But what is it all for? Why does a corporation need to bother with all of this? What difference does it make to success, to share price, to all the things that matter in the company both in the short and long term?

It means everything for an organization. Unless there's a clear driver, a powerful idea, which truly presents the organization in everything it does, it's inevitable that it will only operate tactically; that its component parts will go off in different and sometimes conflicting directions; that each part will focus on the bits that they believe will produce the best results for themselves fastest; and that this fragmentation of focus will, sooner or later, lead to big problems. Whether it's a BP or a Sony, if you lose focus, it will eventually show. And, in the end, it always hits the company where it hurts most – in the share price.

But the issue is much bigger than the fate of the individual corporation. Businesses are only learning slowly that they are part of a world which is under increasingly critical scrutiny. With digital media looking at everything, everywhere, corporations are perfect targets for our dissatisfaction. The world has been shaken by some of the revelations about corporate behaviour. Maybe some corporations have always behaved unscrupulously but we didn't know about it. And now we do. This means that companies are increasingly on the defensive, and, while the reality is that business has genuinely contributed, almost immeasurably, to global wealth and prosperity, corporations don't yet fully understand that they have to make their case clearly and unequivocally. It's not an exaggeration to say that corporations are living in a sceptical, even hostile environment. There's a real case for them to become more imaginative about how they talk and how they act. They need truly to come to terms with a world in which they have a high profile and in which they are expected to make a social contribution.

Over the second half of the 20th century, corporations have increasingly emerged from behind their brands. HSBC took over eighteen major bank brands and changed to a single name; Santander did the same; GE gives virtually all its acquisitions the prefix 'GE'. Corporations like Virgin (and, for that matter, Ryanair) only use one name. This is a difficult issue for organizations like Diageo or LVMH, which, over many years, have acquired product brands with a massive global reputation. It's not very likely that we will ever see Diageo Red or Black label when Johnny Walker is the brand whisky drinkers love. Nevertheless, it's becoming clear that as the corporation, whether it likes it or not, assumes an increasingly high profile publicly, it's going to have to associate itself, one way or another, with its brands. Nestlé, P&G, Unilever and other major corporations have seen this and they are responding. Diageo, as a corporation, promotes 'sensible drinking' on TV, and even the notoriously shy LVMH corporately supports scholarships in design schools. So this is a major issue that the corporation has to think about. How does it emerge publicly? How does it live alongside its brands? And when it does, what is it going to say about itself?

All successful and long-lived entities have pride and self-confidence. I've often cited the military unit as the classic example. Names, uniforms, medals, music, legends and history all underline the pride the unit takes in its achievements and its sense of self-worth. And, in truly successful military units, there are no silos; there is instead a spirit of mutual reliance and support.

Corporations can learn something from this. Plenty of very big corporations have good stories to tell, which are true and positive. Many have much to be proud of. Both Unilever and P&G, for example, have made much of the world cleaner, safer and healthier; they have introduced simple household products – soap, washing powder, toothpaste, and so on – first to Western households, then to poor families in the emerging world, who never had these things before. We are longer-lived and our standards of living are higher because of these companies and others like them. This is true, it's interesting, it's decent. Some of the background, the pioneering stuff, is exciting and, well told, it makes for a good story. And there are plenty of corporations with stories just as good.

Very few corporations make enough of their history. Some corporations have completely forgotten theirs. France Telecom has rechristened itself Orange. So a brand that was created by a branding consultancy in London in 1994 for a Hong Kong company, in order to help nudge itself into a niche in which it had arrived a bit late in the day, has now become the name and brand of one of the largest and most aggressive telecoms companies in Europe. How did that happen? What were the original characteristics of the Orange brand? Have these still been sustained? Do the people within France Telecom who made the change know how to adapt the brand to its extraordinary new role? What are the brand's characteristics now? Is there an historical legacy? And have the people who work for France Telecom been told anything of the history of Orange, of its many vicissitudes? Have they been told the true story of how it got that name in the first place and what it was intended for? In some senses you could claim that the Orange brand has achieved a victory beyond its wildest dreams – but has it? The company should be told. The original actors are still very much alive, and it's an exciting and, in its way, inspiring story.

The story of any large corporation is a significant part of global, social and economic history and it affects people everywhere – customers, staff, recruits, everyone. Organizations like Tata of India, Shell of the Netherlands and Britain, GE of the United States, L'Oréal of France, have remarkable and dramatic stories to tell. Their narrative is an important part of world history. How did Unilever make the world cleaner? How did L'Oréal mass-market seduction? And how did Orange come to replace France Telecom? These stories should give a company's employees and partners pride in continuing a tradition of success.

GE was founded by that eccentric genius, Thomas Alva Edison, arguably the world's most important inventor. GE's story forms a significant part of the growth of American global power and influence. It's fascinating stuff and it's different; it's unique. And the company is still at it, and so are others. Some of the world's greatest medical discoveries come from major pharmaceutical companies. Some of the world's biggest and best companies have traditionally engaged in genuinely exciting and worthwhile socially responsible activities all over the world.

And a few of these corporations are using creatives, film-makers and others, to show what they are doing, how they are doing it, and also to recruit people to do more. It's a huge opportunity, but not enough of them can see it. Corporations,

The Life of
One Little Child

"The Death Street" is what night fatalities named Superior Avenue, Cleveland, before it was transformed, last year, into one of Ohio's safest and best lighted streets.

The electricity costs no more than before the war, the MAZDA lamps much less. With light and the decrease in accidents property values rose.

A supreme investment besides, if it results in saving the life of one little child.

In each district office of the General Electric Company are engineers who are specialists in street lighting. Let them show you how little it costs to have street lights that will increase property values and save lives.

GENERAL ELECTRIC

GE introduces electric street lighting into Cleveland, Ohio, 1926: it was doing Imagineering nearly a century ago!

for the most part, neglect who they are, where they come from, what they did. They should celebrate their history.

However, if a corporation, quite reasonably, wants to talk to a world that's both curious and knowledgeable but also increasingly sceptical, it can tell its own true stories in its own personal style. Social media enable the corporation to tell some of the truths about itself, the great events in which it has taken part, in a compelling, unique and attractive way.

• • •

Interestingly, while the corporate world has been shy to talk about and show itself in an unconventional way and to use the new media dramatically, it is very comfortable with sponsorship, particularly, but not only, of cultural and sporting activities. You can't go to a soccer match (or in India a cricket match) or to the ballet, opera, theatre or an art exhibition without practically drowning in a sea of logos. Corporations support much of the cultural work that goes on in the world.

The corporation understands that sponsorship shows a sense of commitment to society. Sometimes the sponsorship is directly related to what the corporation does – oil companies and Formula One, for example – but quite often it's innovative, warm, charming even, and apparently disinterested: for example, the VW sponsorship of independent cinema in the UK. The corporation is trying to show that it lives beyond immediate self-interest; that it cares about society; even that it has a sense of humour. This is a good beginning, but more corporations need to be involved and they need to be more imaginative. You could almost call it a form of corporate social responsibility.

Apart from a few isolated examples, virtually all companies know they are expected to behave with an appropriate sense of social responsibility, even when this consists of mundane stuff such as disposing of waste carefully or getting decent-quality food into their canteens. But the truth is that, for most, CSR is something they don't really know how to deal with. Can you make money out of it, or is it just a cost without any clear profit benefit at the end of it? Who inside the company knows how to handle it? Which department or division does it fit into? What do you actually do? How do you know how much to spend? Who does it report to? How can you exploit it to your advantage? Is it the same as sponsorship? The whole area is vast and difficult to grasp. Most companies are lost in this maze and their CSR efforts are self-evidently superficial and cosmetic.

Many organizations have CSR departments, with a budget, occasionally quite a big one, sometimes managed with care and good sense, while the rest of the organization goes about its business of making money. But this isn't what CSR is really about. CSR is about an attitude, a way of looking at the world, which is hard to share but which must, if it's going to be truly effective, eventually influence attitudes inside the whole company.

• • •

So what should the well-meaning but ill-informed company do? Strangely enough, one potential solution might lie in outsourcing. Corporations are increasingly outsourcing those activities which are not central to them, or which specialists can do better. Everything you can think of from transport (now, of course, called logistic solutions or – even better – supply chain management) to office cleaning to legal activities is outsourced. So, for some corporations, one way through the CSR dilemma might be to outsource it.

In broad terms, it might look like this. A corporation decides that it is in its long-term interest to demonstrate its commitment to social responsibility. It wants a level of internal engagement but, in addition, it wants to work with an organization dedicated to CSR. So, it talks to charities or NGOs in a related field: for a financial services company it might be an NGO supporting and developing micro-banking. It makes an agreement to support a carefully selected NGO on a long-term basis. In theory, at least, both sides benefit: the NGO gets the long-term financial backing and the management expertise of the corporation; it co-operates with executives seconded from the corporation to develop a high level of professionalism and expertise; and the corporation shares in the halo of making a useful global social contribution, which helps internal morale, recruitment, sales ... and share price.

Take a hypothetical example. We looked at retailing in Chapter 2. What should Zara or H&M do about sourcing? Say to their customers, 'We're going to charge you 10% more for your dress because we have to help raise living standards for Bangladeshi children'? Or should they continue to fudge it? Or should they tell a few lies? Should they just ignore CSR? Or should they outsource it to an NGO or charity that really understands the issues and knows what it's doing – Anti-Slavery International, for example? If they do that, then they can say, 'We are supporting the professionals in this. We want to back them to get it right. We want to give and we want to learn.'

A dreadful accident in a clothing factory in Bangladesh in 2013 with over a thousand deaths is a case in point. Primark and other major retailers, some of whose clothing was made there, were embarrassed and publicly shamed. But what should they have done? Their own employees, their own sourcing people, might have guessed safety standards were appalling but, if the retailers had backed an NGO involved in working conditions inside factories, their position would have been much stronger and, more important, their hands would have been cleaner. Even more important, the tragedy might not have happened.

Of course, there's nothing really new about this idea. You could perhaps say that, at a stretch, the Wellcome Trust, the Ford Foundation, the Tata Trusts and the Rockefeller Foundation are all examples of independent charitable organizations based originally around the corporation outsourcing its CSR. Currently much of the funding of these foundations is, of course, based on shrewd investment but, in some cases, they still have links with their founders.

Bill and Melinda Gates run their own highly efficient, much admired foundation and so do others, like Michael Bloomberg. Then there's the rapidly growing social entrepreneurial activity in which social and environmental issues are treated as business opportunities. There are lots of these and many are very effective, and they are serious and professional.

The Skoll World Forum, arguably the world's leading social entrepreneurial lobbying group, claims to be 'the premier international platform for accelerating entrepreneurial approaches and innovative solutions to the world's most pressing social issues'. It claims disruptive innovations can reshape industries, supplant old technologies and topple political regimes.

There are plenty of business leaders who are also calling for a much more serious commitment to tackling social, environmental and governance issues, and the drive and initiative for all this mostly comes from the society that has led the capitalist model for the last century – the United States of America. There's little doubt that, over the next few years, CSR will become as significant an activity as HR or marketing. CSR is here to stay. So far, despite the hullabaloo, and even though the pace of growth is very rapid, CSR has not yet found a comfortable mainstream place inside the corporation; in most, it's still an add-on. But, whether they like it or not, serious companies will have to deal with CSR in the 21st century. Many may find it difficult, even when times are good, but it will be much harder for them in bad times.

Here's a thought. It might be possible to treat CSR as a contemporary version of the medieval tithe system. The corporation donates a fixed proportion of its profits annually to its NGO partner or partners. The more profit the company makes, the more it contributes to CSR. So the financial success of the corporation and society as a whole are bound together.

This sort of development isn't easy. Both sides, the NGO and the corporation, would find life with each other hard – at first. There would be some mutual suspicion: lots of charities and NGOs don't want to appear to be tainted by too close an association with business, while business executives might perhaps be a bit patronizing about the perceived amateurism of some charities and NGOs.

Nevertheless, a development like this could have a massive impact. Corporations, with all their faults and weaknesses, are familiar with managing things. They know how to get results and how to monitor a proper return on investment. It would mean that, with a strong business culture behind them, CSR activities would be better organized and more effective. Their work would be better monitored. From a corporate point of view it might help businesses to smell a bit sweeter. The boundaries between the worlds of business and global social development would blur, and more socially conscious young people might be attracted to work in the corporate world. One thing is certain: it would mean that ethics courses in business schools would be busier than ever!

Most important, though, if the corporate world was able to deal with CSR at some distance and still derive goodwill from its contribution to social and environmental issues, its own sense of direction would be made clearer. The pretence of trying to carry out two so frequently incompatible objectives simultaneously right inside the corporation would be substantially reduced.

• • •

In the 21st century the world is changing again and the corporation is painfully learning that it has to change with it. The corporation's relationships with society today are much more complex and interlinked than ever before: they are not only about buying and selling, but about acceptance, mutual respect and empathy. This means that CSR is no longer an optional extra. It also means that the corporation has to be much more self-aware and much more coherent than ever before. It must know what it does, how it does it and why it does it, and it has to be coherent because it has to understand that it is operating in a world in which its every action can be scrutinized. So if it is to continue to be successful, it has to project a clear, attractive, unique and authentic personality – and it has to be aligned in everything it does. The corporate brand matters today more than ever.

5

Big Brand Takes Over (or Doesn't).

Dnepropetrovsk is a large industrial city in Eastern Ukraine. It's not outstanding for its wealth or its beauty or its history, or anything much else. In fact, on the face of it, it's a bleak post-Soviet backwater. But it has many of the same shopping malls that you will see in Dallas or Düsseldorf, or, for that matter, most of the world's large cities.

Inside these shopping malls and dotted around the smarter streets (where there are any), you will find Zara, Benetton, McDonald's and the rest of them, all looking alike and selling the same stuff as they do everywhere else in the world. And the families of Dnepropetrovsk, like families everywhere, enjoy strolling about in the summer. The daddies wear T-shirts adorned with huge Nike logos, munch on Snickers and swig from cans of Coke as they check their Blackberrys and iPhones, push their massive baby buggies and gawp at the window displays. And if they don't see whatever they are looking for in the shopping mall or on the High Street, they know they can always look it up online.

In other words, global branding is Big Time in Dnepropetrovsk. And you can reasonably assume that if it's a Big Time brand in Dnepropetrovsk, it's Big Time in more or less every other large city in the world.

So does this mean that Big Brand has finally taken over the globe? Does it confirm what some people have been saying all along, that the world is flat, that it's becoming one huge airport shopping mall and that, whether it's soap or scarves or tablets, you buy the same things anywhere, or you can order them online?

Well, it certainly does look like that, superficially at least. There's increasing homogeneity in the main streets of most big cities in most countries. Of course, there are still a few exceptions. Indian cities, partly because of restrictive laws protecting retailers but also because of the hordes of families all shouting at the tops of their voices, still look different from most places. But even in India, as trading barriers fall, Big Brand is entering the marketplace. I assume North Korea's Pyongyang is different, too, although I haven't been there. But for the most part, at least on the face of it, whether the city is rich or poor, in the West, the East or the emerging South, it seems as though global homogenization is winning ... even in the most dismal of cities.

Or does it? If we look a bit closer, we can see another pattern emerging as well. Does Britain have a Dnepropetrovsk? Maybe it's Hull. Hull was voted the worst city to live in in the UK in 2005.

It has been labelled the obesity capital of England, and spiralling crime rates and poor exam results have seen its policing and education authorities ranked bottom in the country. *'These days, when Hull enters the national consciousness, it's usually as a totem of social deprivation. Few people can match it in the misery stakes,'* says Britain's *Sunday Observer*.[1] But Hull, of course, has its full quota of global brands – River Island, Zara, KFC and the rest of them – even though the city is also a byword for dreary, down-at-heel, poverty-stricken hopelessness.

Interestingly, though, out of the grime something different seems to be emerging – creativity. The *Observer* goes on to say that Hull is attempting an arts and entertainment-based regeneration programme. Hull is looking to become the UK's Capital of Culture in 2017. Hull, it seems, is also looking inside itself to see what it has that's different and attractive and unique. It's exploring its own home-grown talent. And that means unprecedented opportunity for local people.

Hull's creative flair isn't entirely new-found. The city has a major university, whose one-time librarian, Philip Larkin, was one of Britain's most admired poets of the 20th century. It has Truck Theatre, the Ferens Art Gallery and other local-based arts attractions. 'There are 300 bands in Hull,' notes Mikey Scott, who runs a recording studio. 'It's ridiculous that no one knows this.' What's really astonishing is that there appears to be so much talent in this one traditional, neglected city.

Derry in Northern Ireland is another interesting example. It was the UK's Capital of Culture in 2013, its strength based around the economic success of the Republic of Ireland just down the road. But when Ireland's economy collapsed, so did Derry's. The statistics for joblessness and child poverty were shocking. According to Ilex, the urban renewal agency, 35% of Derry's children live in poverty.[2] But depressed Derry is fighting back, by mixing technology (not all of it cutting-edge) with the arts. As *The Economist* has noted:[3]

'*Local firms with a digital connection range from a unit of America's Seagate, which has invested £700m ($1.1 billion) in a plant making hard-drive parts and is the city's biggest private employer, to tiny start-ups like Rotor, in which a recent graduate, Diarmuid Moloney, helps new bands to make music videos. The showpieces of digital culture include Dog Ears, a maker of animated films and apps for children, and 360 Production, which makes history and archaeological broadcasts.*

'*For a week in September [2013], Derry will play host to thousands of creative and digitally-minded types for a networking event known as CultureTech....*'

And if there's that much talent in Hull and in Derry, too, how much undiscovered talent is there everywhere else in the world, including Dnepropetrovsk?

Even while Big Brand continues to thrive and grow, this story of remarkable creative activity and renewal is being played out all over the place, including in many of the most deprived cities in the world. You can find it everywhere.

Detroit, once the global capital of automobile manufacture and the home of Motown, fell to pieces as the US auto industry collapsed in the last quarter of the 20th century. The city went officially bankrupt in July 2013 and has become a byword for chaos, crime, deprivation and depopulation. Its inner city is deserted and has become a criminal, druggy battleground. Between 2000 and 2010 its population dropped by 25%,[4] and it will soon be under 700,000 for the first time in a century. Unemployment is more than twice the national average, and the city has the highest violent crime and murder rate in the United States. Even in Detroit, however, there are signs that the city is changing. Young creative groups are rebuilding decayed areas, turning them into artists' quarters. The city is beginning to show signs of new life, as innovators with very little money but a lot of ideas attempt to revive and renew it.

This kind of thing is happening all over, whether pop-up shops or new kinds of places to go to that are restaurants but simultaneously galleries and theatres. All sorts of new, exciting ideas are emerging everywhere, especially perhaps where you wouldn't expect. Paradoxically, as big cities become more homogenous the world over, they are also becoming more individual and more different from each other. This seems to be especially true of the cities that have been through precipitous decline or trauma.

Berlin is perhaps the outstanding example. No city in the world has been through more dramatic change, both in perception and reality. From the Kaiser's triumphalist, militaristic Berlin at the turn of the 20th century to the rowdy, louche cabaret Berlin of the 1920s and early '30s; to Hitler's murderous Third Reich Berlin; to devastated, post-war, divided, threatened and threatening Berlin; to Cold War East and West Berlin – two cities, a concept almost unimaginable to anyone under thirty years old today. And now look at Contemporary Berlin. It has emerged as a leading European creative hub, one of the most exciting cities in the world – yet another manifestation of Berlin, attracting brilliant young talent from everywhere.

And all this means we are living in a strange time for branding. While, on the one hand, Big Brands are becoming more powerful and ubiquitous and they are both homogenizing and connecting the world, on the other hand new brands, created by courageous young entrepreneurs, are popping up absolutely everywhere. They are complementary to, and sometimes competitive with, Big Brands. They are the flag-bearers of heterogeneity.

• • •

The opportunity to create something new, different and exciting embraces ideas around products and services, as well as the arts. The entrepreneurial spirit has never been more potent. If you're a young person with a creative idea in music, art or theatre or business of almost any kind – retail, product, service – there has never been a better time. Individuals with talent have more opportunity than ever before.

How does it happen? Partly because people everywhere are better connected through social media. And it also happens because social media provide outlets for individual intuition and the creative instinct. You have the opportunity; you get an idea; you develop it; it works (you hope); you create a name and a visual identity. So now you have a brand. You put it on a website and you use the internet and other social media, so people see it. You don't need conventional advertising, which is expensive and much of which has no clear focus anyway. You don't necessarily need much money, at least to start with. Social media are so fragmented, so self-generating and so self-selecting that if you do it right, someone, somewhere, will notice. The potential audience is vast and the cost of a product launch is low. The opportunities for exposure have never been greater and the barriers never lower. You know pretty soon if you have a potential success.

And then you get funding – maybe from 'friends and family', as they say; or crowdfunding on the internet; or a private equity firm (there are plenty of those swimming around, hungry for the chance to invest, build, make money and get out). And then, if you're really successful, you get bought by one of the Big Brands which likes the idea, because they see that it will work for them; that they can grow it and make money out of it. Big Brands will call it 'adding value'.

Many of the new players with new brands are amusingly ingenious. Just browse the web and you will find some of them:

- Method is a 'super-environmentally friendly' brand of cleaning products and soaps. It claims its packaging is made of plastic collected from empty bottles floating about in the ocean.
- Sugru, 'a self-setting rubber for fixing, modifying and improving your stuff' (as it defines itself on its website) was developed by an Irish entrepreneur in the UK. It's a silicon rubber product (a clay that freezes), used to fix broken things, almost any dry material, and is very easy to use – even for clumsy people. It also claims to be waterproof and dishwasher-safe.
- GiffGaff is a UK-based mobile phone operator, run by its members in exchange for customer support and brand promotion; it's just much cheaper.
- Square is an electronic payment device that allows you to make payments by credit card through a mobile phone.

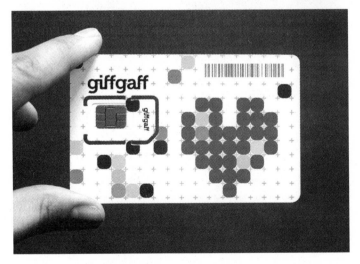

New ideas; new brands.

- Zipcar is a car rental service. You pay an annual fee for membership and then use their cars anytime and anywhere, paying by the hour. Cars are scattered around the city and there's a map showing which ones are closest to you. You return the car to its reserved bay so there's no parking issue. It's called 'car sharing', because people can use a car whenever and wherever they want, without the problems and responsibilities of owning one.
- Whitelines is a Swedish company that has created a new kind of writing paper. Instead of having black lines on a white background, their notebooks have white lines on a light grey background; much easier and more fun to use.

There are thousands of these new product ideas, bursting out all over the internet and promoted through social media and word of mouth. I've just picked a few, more or less at random. The ideas come from all over the world. Some are dotty. Most are ingenious. Many have a strong social content. A few are quite extraordinary. 'Why didn't I think of that? It's so obvious. Amazing!' Most of the new brands will, of course, fizzle out, but a few will be very successful and some that do well will eventually morph by acquisition into Big Brands. And then the cycle will start all over again.

How does all this impact on us consumers? What are we looking for? Well, as usual, we're a bit mixed up. We want to be like everyone else, buying Big Brands, Nike, Adidas and all that, and we also want to be different – to distinguish ourselves, to individuate, to show off our personal tastes. This means that, in an homogenized world, there's a big opportunity for niche products and services. Sometimes these can be big niches that newer, smaller players can carve out with individual products and services. The paradox is that, as Big Brands get bigger, this creates more room for niches. There's opportunity everywhere you look.

Kaya Sorhaindo of Six Scents, a perfume company, told the *New York Times*: '*The celebrity and big-brand fragrances are too calculated.... Consumers want self-discovery, and not us trying to dictate some story.*'[5] So he, among others, introduced a new perfume brand, one of many that keep popping up. There are now plenty of perfumes with 'a hint of Arabia', 'a touch of the Mughal', perfumes from 'the world's heart – London'. Ormonde Jayne is one of these new small perfume companies, selling very special and particular scents at Harrods, online and in little boutiques.

Local foods, furniture, jewelry, textiles, ceramics: industries like these encourage more creativity. Just go to a degree show at a great art or design school, like Central St Martin's in London, and be amazed at the level of ingenuity. And people get especially excited if it's made locally and seems authentic. According to Tyler Brûlé, editor-in-chief of Monocle, Heath Ceramics – a business that makes and sells its products in Sausolito, San Francisco – can't keep the crowds away. Why? Partly because they like the look and feel of the ceramics, partly because these are designed and made on the spot.

You can find this kind of development in every field. Bright people look for the gap. In hotels, Hilton, Holiday Inn and at the upper end Four Seasons are ubiquitous brands offering exactly the same reassuring levels of service wherever you go, but if you want to be a bit different you can stay in almost any city at a boutique hotel designed 'for the more discriminating'; a hotel where the concierge knows the city better than the locals, where the ingredients on the menu are local, and where the place feels authentic. The more Big Brands dominate, the more opportunity there is for newer brands with new ideas to emerge and compete and (sometimes) win.

Homogeneity and heterogeneity are competing with each other, and are also complementary to each other, everywhere, in goods and services. While the world of the Big Brands is getting bigger and more risk-averse, the new, small brands are getting cleverer, cheekier and more daring.

There's a fundamental difference in the way that traditional Big Brands and the new, small, smart brands work. Big Brands win on size and power; Big Brands work on research, on numbers and on all kinds of data drivers and analytics, epitomized by IBM in its advertising:[6]

'Using analytics, not instinct.
'Executives long relied on intuition to formulate strategy and assess risk. Such thinking is rendered obsolete by Big Data.

'Today, when each individual is connected with millions of others, the cost of a bad call can be devastating. Analytics helps leaders see beyond their own biases to find real patterns and anticipate events.'

Grant Duncan of Spencer Stuart says in *The Economist*: *'The next generation of marketers may not be able to be as intuitive and creatively inspiring as their predecessors.'*[7] Well, you can certainly say that again. Brands in big organizations are increasingly managed by MBA-trained marketing people, who tend to regard numbers in the same way babies feel about pacifiers: they are both comforting and reassuring.

None of this is new. Marketing people have always been torn between emotion, intuition and instinct on the one hand and apparently rational analysis on the other. In the world of Big Brands it's clear that, in this long-term battle, right now analytics is on top. The quantity of data available is vast and its analysis can be more or less instantaneous and continuous so that, in theory, marketing people can learn almost at once what works and what doesn't by looking at reactions on a screen. Focus groups look at new proposed ideas and products, consumer behaviour and purchasing patterns are scrutinized on screen and in real time, and nothing is launched until it's very thoroughly researched – to death, you might say.

But how much real use is all this research and analysis? At one level it's very valuable. It's very important to know what makes people buy. But in the end, data, however much you analyze it, cannot truly predict: it cannot tell you what to do, it cannot tell you what will work in the future. Shakespeare didn't check out *Hamlet* with a focus group. Steve Jobs didn't launch Apple's big breakthrough using research. That's why most breakthroughs come from small, new brands – working on hunch.

Of course, I quite understand that analyzing what is happening now really does help and I am all in favour of it, and analyzing what went right and why is also very valuable. Even more important, in my experience, is analyzing what went wrong and why. You really learn a lot from that. The problems start when you rely on research to try to tell you what will happen in the future. This, in all my experience, mostly doesn't work. For the most part, people don't know what they want until they see it, and many are not even sure then.

When I was Chairman of Wolff Olins, the branding consultancy that created the mobile phone brand, Orange, in London back in 1994, all the focus groups told my colleagues who were running the project not to call the brand Orange. 'Why Orange? What are you talking about? Why not Banana?' Now France Telecom, its current owner (it has had three), has finally realized what it has bought and, as I pointed out in Chapter 4, has rechristened its entire organization Orange. So, maybe Orange was not such a silly name after all.

Let me be clear. I am not suggesting that data, analysis and all the rest of it has no place; nor am I suggesting that the only thing that matters is intuition and creativity, although anybody who knows anything about life knows that all the big decisions you make, who you love and marry, how many children you have, where you live, the way you live, are based around gut instinct. What I am saying is that an appropriate balance between heart and head brings about the most effective results, and that, right now, Big Brand is relying far too much on analysis and not enough on intuition, and that's why it's insufficiently innovative.

· · ·

It's hardly surprising that, since quantification, ratings, analytics and all the rest of it are becoming increasingly central to the way the corporation examines its world, it also wants to quantify the value of its own brands and demonstrate that what it spends on its brands is repaid a thousand-fold in their financial value. Hence brand valuation.

There are two factors at work here. The first is that there are league tables for almost everything – soccer clubs, universities, quality of life in cities, the hundred richest people in the world. We love league tables. Business schools are rated No. 1 to No. 100, based particularly around how much their alumni can earn on graduation and similar academic distinctions. Virtually every L'Oréal advertisement on television tells you that 94 women out of 100 believe that the particular skin potion being promoted makes them look 15.5 years younger – 'so they're worth it'. So why shouldn't there be a league table for how much the world's greatest brands are worth?

And the second factor is that we all look for the magic formula that reveals the truth. 'Humanity,' says the leading economist Samuel Brittan in *The Financial Times*, 'will never cease its futile search for magic numbers'.[8] Brittan is talking in his piece about how professors of economics always purport to have the one true formula, which is invariably revealed as wrong. 'A Quixotic quest' and 'spell of magic numbers' is what Brittan calls it. And it mesmerizes the big companies with their massive brands. And, of course, the more the brand appears to be worth, the more brand managers can justify their budgets ... so everyone joins in the game.

In 2011, *The Economist* published the results of a study carried out by a couple of researchers in the Netherlands which seemed to prove what most of us already know – that we not only buy designer labels like Tommy Hilfiger or Lacoste because we like the look and feel of them but also because we like the status they confer on us.[9] This research is entertaining but hardly groundbreaking.

There's a really interesting bit that comes next, though, which is to do with the value of the brand. How much should we pay for it? *The Economist* says: '*A work of art's value, for example, can change radically, depending on who is believed to have created it, even though the artwork itself is unchanged. And people will willingly buy counterfeit goods, knowing they are knock-offs, if they bear the right label.'* In other words: brands matter, and what you are prepared to pay for them is what you perceive they are worth.

This is a grand way of saying that people are prepared to pay much more for the T-shirt that says 'Made in Italy' than for the one that says 'Made in Turkey'. Or more for a T-shirt with a crocodile label than for one with a polo pony, even if nobody can spot differences in quality. Status is transferred, as *The Economist* puts it, to the label.

So how much is the label – whatever it is – worth? How much should you pay for it? The answer is surely: whatever it's worth to you at any given moment. There cannot be an objective value to something so personal. You bought that dress for £900, you loved the label, you wore it once but now you don't like it; the label isn't so fashionable anymore, you've gone off the designer. For you – it's worthless.

The brand's value, in other words, is entirely in the eyes of the beholder. So where does so-called objective brand valuation come into this equation? Using complex and, to me, entirely incomprehensible but apparently objective econometric measurements, a number of organizations claim to be able to give accurate measurements of the value of a brand – often of a corporate brand. They can not only tell you what the corporate brand is worth today compared with yesterday but they can also calculate, over the years, your brand's value compared with others, frequently in areas of activity that are entirely unrelated to each other.

What makes this brand-ranking business somewhat self-undermining is that the various brand valuation organizations competing against each other offer up wildly different figures for the brands they are purporting to quantify so precisely. As Mark Ritson pointed out in *Marketing Week*, Intel is given 8th, 20th and 49th place, depending on which rating company you look at.[10] Hermès is given 32nd, 63rd or 321st. Here are some more anomalies for 2012 ratings:

- Samsung: 9th (Interbrand), 55th (BrandZ), 6th (Brand Finance)
- Visa: 74th (Interbrand), 15th (BrandZ), not listed by Brand Finance
- Disney: 13th (Interbrand), 43rd (BrandZ), 50th (Brand Finance)
- Tiffany: not listed by Interbrand or Brand Finance, 52nd (BrandZ).

No wonder some of us are a bit sceptical. On the other hand, brands are intangibles that do have value. Whether Coke, Apple, Mercedes-Benz, Disney or Virgin, for many companies their brand or brands are worth much more than all the rest of the business put together, so to ignore their value on a balance sheet is absurd. But, in reality, any brand valuation is not much more than a sometimes, though not always, well-informed guess.

All this must be extremely comforting for those organizations whose main value resides in their brand or brands and other intangibles. It makes their balance sheet look healthy, and it gives their senior executives a feeling of relaxed self-confidence when they talk to investors. It is also – and now I am searching for a way to put this politely – hot air.

What do these numbers, these so-called metrics, actually mean in real life? Anything can affect share price: Eurozone financial problems, American political problems, shifty behaviour from senior executives, phone hacking in a newspaper you happen to own, a blow-out in an oil field, a batch of nasty stuff in soft drinks – anything. The current, apparently endless financial crisis should underline and emphasize all that.

And what this means is that the value of a corporate brand or a product brand is both volatile and subjective, and it embraces a whole world of political, social, cultural, economic, financial and physical uncertainties.

The fundamental issue is whether quantification based on a level of apparent certainty represents any kind of reality, or whether it just allows one to feel comfortable. I believe that many people are quite deluded by the information that numbers attempt to convey. Figures like these try to quantify the unquantifiable, to give the illusion of certainty to something that's essentially uncertain – which is the way we all think, feel, react and emote.

So don't trust so-called objective brand valuation, and just remember a brand is worth only what someone is prepared to pay for it. And that applies to a T-shirt or a painting, or, as we found out a few years ago, Lehman Brothers.

It is perhaps worth bearing in mind that it was the Gaussian copula – the precise formula worked out by the-then mathematical geniuses who worked for the hedge funds – that killed Wall Street just a few years ago. These geniuses couldn't be wrong because the formula was so precise and foolproof, but, as it subsequently turned out, they were.

• • •

I have digressed into the world of brand valuation simply because it underlines how significant brands are becoming in the 21st century. We are now living in a world in which a brand can emerge in any area of activity, and we are beginning to realize how valuable these brands can become. As every field of endeavour – commerce, sport, education, research, social entrepreneurship – becomes more global, so more high-profile and more competitive brands emerge.

Universities all over the world are competing with each other to attract the world's best talent both in teaching and research … and students. So what do they have to do to show they are in the race? Create strong, attractive brands, of course. The *Times Higher Education* has a 'world university rankings' list. If you are in the top fifty you attract the best teachers and students. OK, if academics are uncomfortable with the 'brand' word, they can say 'reputation' instead.

The extraordinary success of the arts and, in particular, galleries, museums, opera and ballet companies, is largely a function of the brands they have developed. Guggenheim Bilbao, is, of course, the classic example. Although there are Guggenheims in four cities, it's the Bilbao Guggenheim that helped to change perceptions of Bilbao. It's not so much what's inside the museum that people talk about; it's the outside that matters. It's the Frank Gehry building that has been the catalyst which has rebranded the city. As *The Guardian* noted: '*The mayor of Bilbao [was] named World Mayor of the Year 2012, in recognition of the city's transformation into a worldwide arts hub. [He] is credited with using … Guggenheim … to turn declining industrial Bilbao into a cultural centre.*'[11] In other words, the Guggenheim arts brand has helped to turn Bilbao into a destination city brand.

And these big gallery brands have, for the first time ever, created popular excitement around the idea of art. There is now a plethora of galleries in Bilbao, all thriving on the Guggenheim brand. And it becomes self-perpetuating. In Britain both Tate and the V&A have turned museums and galleries into popular entertainments – a staggering achievement. The V&A, one of the world's most successful museums, now attracts more than three million visitors per year. Museums and galleries are no longer places where only middle-class, middle-aged professionals go. They are part of a wider, more inclusive world. Galleries are popular, even populist institutions. More people go to museums in the UK than go to soccer matches![12] This would simply not have been possible without powerful, clever, consistent branding.

It's the same story in theatres, opera and ballet companies. At Sadler's Wells, the ballet and theatre organization that runs a ballet school and a number of theatres, the brand has real power. Brand is in charge of communication, marketing, publications, multi-media, press, PR – even ticketing.

It is now a truism to say that Britain's best-known brand worldwide is Manchester United. We all know that soccer is a brand-led business. Is it branding that has made the sport into a global business, or is it the other way round? Probably a bit of both. In India, it's cricket. In the United States, it's American football. The teams that comprise these sports are all massive brands. And the social infrastructure in which we all live and on which we all depend thrives on this kind of continual brand creation, death and rebirth in unlikely spheres and places.

• • •

One of the most important and influential areas into which branding is now moving is corporate social responsibility (CSR) – and it's arguably the most significant. As NGOs and charities on the one hand, and businesses on the other, cautiously nudge up to each other, and as the social entrepreneurial corporations that link the two areas become increasingly influential, they all have to think about their brand. In principle, of course, charities and NGOs are perfect subjects for brands and branding because they are about empathy. The more effectively a charity brands itself, the more highly successful it's likely to be.

Traditionally many charities have been unsympathetic to branding, because it seems 'commercial' and 'phoney'; it appears, in some way, to undermine the high-mindedness of the organization. This quaintly contrarian point of view is now slowly disappearing and charities and, perhaps more particularly NGOs, are learning that the more clearly and attractively they present themselves to their various publics, or – put another way – the more effectively and professionally they brand themselves, the more successful they will be.

As issues around CSR become more high-profile, the NGO/charity has to stop thinking of business as the enemy and start a dialogue leading to partnership, while the corporation has to stop treating CSR as something it does on Tuesdays through the medium of its little CSR department and try to work out how, through partnership, being socially useful to society becomes a component part of all its activities.

Does this mean that NGOs need to become more like businesses? Well, yes, in the sense that they need to be managed professionally with clear goals and, where possible, measurable outcomes. And certainly, yes, in the sense that they need to have a clear idea of who they are, what they are trying to do, why they are trying to do it and who all their audiences, internal and external, are likely to be. And above all, yes, because when they know all that, they will understand that they need to develop powerful brands to get and sustain the support they need.

As all this works its way through the system, it's perfectly possible, even likely, that over the next few generations, bright young graduates will see a career that spans conventional business in a large organization and a few years in an NGO as the norm. Moving from one activity to another will be part of a professional career pattern.

When brands and branding enter the world of the NGO, what it should mean, and usually does, is that the organization becomes more professional and effective and underlines its moral compass, because it achieves more.

• • •

As branding moves through the 21st century, it creates an exciting mixture of increasing competition and increasing opportunity. Big Brand keeps on growing but small, entrepreneurial brands pop up all over the place, continually finding the opportunities that Big Brands, with all their data analysis, miss.

In all areas of activity – education, sport, health, the arts, culture, charities, social entrepreneurship and, of course, in the Big Business world itself – there are an increasing number of organizations overlapping and competing for talent, for finance, for a high profile, for success. It's happening on a scale that nobody has ever seen before because globalization and social media have, between them, created this extraordinary climate. Anyone can promote anything, and the brand is the medium they use. Branding on this scale is unprecedented, certainly in my quite long lifetime in the branding world.

6

New Brands From Everywhere.

In the 18th century the West fell in love with the Orient – well, anyway, with Oriental products: porcelain, silk, cotton and other fabrics and furniture. In the 21st century the West is doing it all over again, only it's called growth markets now and, this time, the speed and scale of it all dwarfs everything that went before.

In 2004, the V&A Museum in London mounted a vast exhibition called 'Encounters' – that is, encounters between European and Oriental cultures. Relationships were based around an unlikely mix of mutual suspicion and admiration. Oriental rulers were fascinated by Western technology; Westerners, on the other hand, were enthralled by the luxury products of the Orient. As the exhibition catalogue put it: 'In the period from 1500 to 1800 Asians and Europeans often met as equals. Indeed at centres of dominance ... the encounter took place on Asian terms.'[1]

Then it all changed. The West grew stronger, the East weaker. As power shifted, attitudes shifted too. The Europeans became colonizers, the Asians colonized. The West saw itself as culturally and technologically dominant. Western technological supremacy coincided with and certainly hastened the decline and fall of the great Eastern powers. In India the Moghul Empire fell apart from a mix of internal and external pressures to which the British and French enthusiastically contributed. Following decades of struggle, the Moghuls were replaced by Britain as the paramount power, initially acting through the transparent veneer of its commercial surrogate, the East India Company. After a variety of disturbances and a major civil war, or rebellion, or mutiny (depending on which historical interpretation you choose), the Company's rule was disposed of. In 1876, Disraeli created Queen Victoria Empress of India, no doubt on his own initiative; certainly nobody else was asked, not least the peoples of India. This froze cultural attitudes between the victors and the defeated. The British were on top, so their education system, their language, their law, justice and technology became the admired model. As part of this baggage, so did products made in the West. Tea, cotton, jute and other raw materials came from India, but finished products came from the West. The Indian cotton industry was destroyed and Lancashire triumphed.

The situation in China was somewhat messier. China was never completely conquered or colonized, although chunks of it were taken over by Western powers. There were colonies, such as Hong Kong, and territories, euphemistically called Treaty Ports, run by Russians, French and Germans. There are still a few strange hangovers from that period around (Tsingtao beer, a current Chinese product, comes from a city once called Tientsin, a former German Treaty Port; the beer was originally brewed for the Germans living there).

There was not much that Europe made that China wanted, although Europeans imported Chinese silk and tea and other products. So the trading deficit was eventually solved by massive exports to China of Indian-grown opium. When the Chinese protested, the European powers dealt with this impudent restraint of trade by force. The various Opium Wars of the 19th century, all of which China of course lost, were fought to introduce and sustain opium exports from British-run India to China. So perhaps we shouldn't be too surprised if the Chinese governments of the 21st century are less than fastidious in their behaviour in Africa and elsewhere. We know who they learnt it from and how.

Of the major East Asian powers, only Japan escaped total despoliation. Her turn came a bit later. All of this activity and conquest not only completely changed the balance of military and political power between East and West, it also changed attitudes and the balance of cultural and economic dominance. In crude terms, as the West became richer and more powerful, it developed an apparently unshakeable belief in its innate superiority. It was not just that Western races (as they were called) thought they were cleverer and physically stronger, Westerners considered their culture profoundly superior in every respect. To get a whiff of all this, just read 19th- and early 20th-century adventure yarns by writers like G. A. Henty or Sapper or John Buchan, or Rudyard Kipling, although it's clear he was somewhat ambivalent about it all. As late as the 1930s Biggles

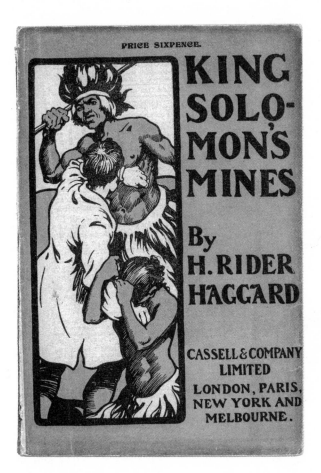

Western superiority challenged,
1885...

was always 'biffing the natives' about. Assumptions of Western ethnic superiority were sustained right through the first half of the 20th century and only began to disappear with the end of colonial empires after World War II.

• • •

This white supremacy ideology coincided with the development of mass marketing. From the late 19th century onwards, in the West, the combination of more or less universal literacy, higher standards of living for the working class, and massive improvements in transport and distribution systems led to the growth of cheap daily newspapers and then, directly, to the beginnings of a consumer society. Mass-market consumer brands began to emerge in most Western countries. These became an intrinsic part of Western life. The time and place where modern consumer branding began is very significant, as it accounts for the apparently effortless and total dominance of Western brands in the world marketplace until the end of the 20th century.

For the last 150 years or so, certainly since the late 19th century until the end of the 20th century, the High Street – any High Street anywhere in the West – has been dominated by brands, ordinary fast moving consumer brands as well as luxury brands, almost all originating in Western society with a Western cultural background. Until very recently, virtually everything that came in a can or a carton or a paper wrapper, from cereals to soup to washing powder, was a product of Western culture and Western lifestyle. The huge companies that produced those goods, initially of course for domestic consumption, were based in Western countries, at first the United States but also Western Europe. Brands – from P&G, Colgate, General Foods, Kraft and the others from the United States, to Cadbury and Lever from the United Kingdom, Henkel from Germany, Nestlé from Switzerland, Danone from France, and so on – dominated the shelves, first of grocery shops and then of supermarkets, primarily in Western marketplaces for over a hundred years.

That's how Western mass-market products – and the advertising, marketing and branding with which they were accompanied – accidentally, but inevitably, became part of the West's baggage of cultural superiority. Over decades Western consumer products were loaded into the cargo holds of the ships of the imperial powers and shipped to their colonies. Lever, the predecessor of the Unilever organization, started operations in India – at that time, of course, the jewel in the crown of the British Empire – as early as 1888 and began manufacturing there in 1933. Hindustan Lever, as it became (and subsequently Hindustan Unilever), introduced Western products such as soap and toothpaste, first to the expatriate European community and then, as they became richer and more influenced by Western lifestyles, to the more prosperous and assimilated sectors of the indigenous population. So, in India, toothpaste became a mark of cultural hierarchy and assimilation as it slowly replaced the neem stick.

The same story applies in luxury products, only more so. In the 1920s and '30s, no Maharajah felt complete without a small or, for that matter, a large fleet of Rolls-Royce or Lanchester cars and a whole selection of other trinkets, baubles and luxury showpieces of the West.

Put another way, alongside Western political dominance there was a cultural dominance which expressed itself in an uncritical admiration of everything the West could offer, linked to a disdain for most of what the colonies themselves produced. That stuff was for poorer, less educated people. Inevitably, a plethora of Western brands of every kind, from the cheapest and most utilitarian to the most ostentatious and extravagant, all dominated the Oriental marketplace and pushed local products into second, third and fourth place.

This legacy of Western dominance ran deep and, although it's under intense challenge today, still remains. It explains why, when McDonald's first opened in emerging markets, crowds queued outside for hours waiting to savour the delights of the experience. It also explains why young Japanese women are still so obsessed by Louis Vuitton. It goes at least some way towards explaining why, according to legend, a popular drink among rich young people in Shanghai is Petrus laced with Coca-Cola. It explains why Bentley, Ferrari, Lamborghini and all the expensive German cars do so well: they are the direct descendants of the luxury cars of the 1920s and '30s. In other words, it explains why Western-inspired luxury products are still so coveted in Southern and Eastern Asia. The mindset, inculcated over more than two hundred years, is 'West is Best'.

• • •

That mindset is still hanging about. By implication, whatever it was, if it came from Europe or America it was better. So what could local entrepreneurs do? One way forward for a local manufacturer was to mimic the Western product. Thums Up was a fizzy drink created by an Indian company for the Indian marketplace, following the expulsion of multinationals like

Coca-Cola by a 1970s Socialist government worried about the establishment of monopolies. Thums Up was, of course, a direct imitation of a Western branded fizzy drink and, in its day, it gave Coke and Pepsi a good run for its money. It must have been successful because Coca-Cola now owns it. By the 1980s there were plenty of companies in India selling low-priced, Indian-made, imitation-Western products with labels that purported to be European (often Italian for clothes). Many clothes stores in India back then stocked leather jackets with labels like Bammbinno or McLoud and Fraser (I've made those up). But, even as I write this, the major Indian textile group SKNL markets brands with names like Reid & Taylor and Belmonte. Among these kinds of companies there is still an inclination to disguise slightly the Indian origins of their brands.

Thums Up: India's top fizzy drink.

An alternative direction for the local manufacturer was to ignore Western competition and Western brands, stick to traditional products and market them in the traditional way. Of the many local manufacturers who continued to make local products with local characteristics for local consumption, many remained unbranded. For example, *beedis*, a very cheap unbranded cigarette-type product, competed on price and within a restricted geographic area with the cheapest Indian cigarette brands from the aptly named Imperial Tobacco Company.

Meanwhile, the traditional luxury goods business of India and China continued to exist, but in tiny niches for a very small, discriminating market. Of course, there was also a plethora of hand-made, hand-loomed, Gandhi-inspired textiles, but – although they were frequently very beautiful, high quality and had considerable political and symbolic significance – they were marginal in terms of market share and commercial influence.

Most manufacturers in emerging markets took the third and easiest route. They made, and still make, products designed by and for a Western company and carrying a Western brand name. These manufacturers are simply anonymous suppliers to Gap, Nike, Marks & Spencer and the rest. Now that 'country of origin' labelling is becoming increasingly important, Western companies are having to acknowledge that local suppliers exist. Many products that you buy in supermarkets bear the legend 'Made in China' somewhere or other in very small type, and Apple's iPod rather disdainfully reads, 'Designed by Apple in California. Assembled in China'. This is still by far the largest sector in the emerging markets. We make. You brand.

However, the situation is now beginning to change. Relatively recently and, as an indication of the beginnings of some sort of self-confidence, local manufacturers are starting to make imitations of Western products but with local brand names, which, with increasing enthusiasm, they promote. According to *The Financial Times*: '*Li Ning, the domestic sportswear brand named after the Olympic gymnast who lit the flame at the opening ceremony of the Beijing Olympic Games ...has pulled neck and neck with Adidas as the number two sports brand after Nike in China, a move which could mark a seminal moment in the history of innovation and a sign that China can rebrand itself as not just cheap, but cool.*'[2] 'But,' the FT goes on to say, '*it is uncertain whether Chinese companies are ready to compete head to head on branding, marketing, innovation, design and quality with some of the strongest brands on earth.*' And, of course, the Li Ning product doesn't come from an indigenous cultural background: it is a Chinese imitation of a Western cultural artifact – the smelly sports shoe.

A modulation of this development is also tentatively emerging. Companies are continuing to make products based around Western archetypes but positively underlining their national provenance as an advantage. I once worked for a tyre manufacturer in India who wanted to break into the European marketplace. I advised the company to emphasize its Indian origins. The basis of this argument ran: 'If we can make tyres for the worst drivers in the world, on the worst roads in the world, then we can certainly make tyres for you in Europe.'

• • •

So things are changing, but very slowly. For very many years – in fact, for nearly two centuries – the West's superiority was also manifested, not only in marketing and promotion, but in technology. When Japan was opened up to the rest of the world, courtesy of the American Commodore Perry and his fleet of 'black ships' in 1853, there was no overt Western military conquest. What followed was a particularly bloody era of civil war, now known as the Meiji restoration, in which the influence of the traditional samurai class was effectively destroyed. After that, although Japan was not directly colonized, it became the West's most devoted and adept pupil. Japan copied the West, particularly in technology. The Japanese took the best that they could find from everywhere. Their navy was based on Britain's, their army on Germany's. In 1904–5 Japan proved that it could adopt Western technology so effectively that it won a short, sharp war against Russia, a major European power.

So what was the result of the huge Japanese success? The Japanese became the biggest and most successful mimics of Western products. The great Japanese companies, the *zaibatsu*, went into emulation mode on a grand scale. In the first half of the 20th century Japanese products of every kind became a byword for imitations, usually cheap and inferior, of Western models. It was only after World War II that Japanese manufacturers learned about innovation and quality and branding, and that's when they began to develop the high reputation their products have today. As Japanese companies began to develop more self-confidence, they started to use Japanese brand names and they began to innovate, in some cases overtaking Western models. It took something like forty years before Japanese companies could compete on quality and reputation head to head with Western companies.

South Korean companies started later and are doing it quicker, although even today Korean products still almost always sell against Japanese competition on price. Kia and Hyundai are not quite Toyota or Honda, but they are nearly there. There's no doubt, though, that Samsung has arrived.

And now, as I write this, China is moving through the same series of phases. As mentioned earlier, currently most Chinese manufacturers simply make unbranded products for Western corporations. They make it for two dollars, sell it to Western corporations for five dollars, the Western corporation sticks its brand name on and sells it to the customer for fifteen or even fifty dollars. Chinese companies are just beginning to get the idea that, if they develop powerful brands themselves, they might keep some of that profit. Or, as the quaint marketing phrase goes, they may 'add more value' ... to themselves, of course. But they are only just learning and they still tend to emulate. If a Chinese company makes a classy product, it's often qualified by a Western association or a Western-style name. Most have not yet developed sufficient self-confidence to go further.

With all this as background it's hardly surprising that most companies in emerging economies making products based around local cultural patterns have been tentative about moving into international markets, because this is really a giant step forward for them.

• • •

I believe, however, that we are now at a turning point. Although Western cultural patterns still predominate, we are beginning to see a profound shift. In one sense, we are moving back to an 18th-century mindset when things from 'Over There' were exotic and attractive. The change has only just started and momentum is still beginning to build. And since this is the 21st century, we are not only talking about products that you buy over the counter.

The newly emerging markets are just beginning to develop sufficient self-confidence to create and brand products and services developed from their own indigenous cultures and they are even starting to market them across the world. Put bluntly, as the political hegemony of the West declines, the cultural hegemony declines with it. It's all very new, a bit tentative, and it varies greatly between different sectors.

In 2008, the movie *Slumdog Millionaire* won eight Oscars and became a huge global success. It's a fairly typical Bollywood story: handsome hero and beautiful heroine, who do one huge dance number right at the end, eventually defeat quite a few nasty people including, unusually, members of the Mumbai police and a game show host. Quite a lot of the dialogue is in

English and everything works out fine in the end. There's an important story behind the story, though. For the first time ever, a more or less Bollywood product broke through into the global marketplace. It's true that the script was written by one Englishman and the film was directed by another, but – and this is key – it was designed for Western as well as Indian audiences. The eight Oscars can be seen not so much as an award to a particular movie as Hollywood's recognition that there is another, quite different but equally powerful movie culture that will over time take its place alongside Hollywood itself among movie-going audiences all over the world.

Slumdog Millionaire is an important harbinger and it has been followed by a trickle of others. It is a signal that in entertainment, as well as in a lot of other fields, the traditional dominance and the admired model that Western culture represents is being challenged. The multi-polarity that has become a reality in the world of politics is also emerging in our daily lives, in our cultural experiences. This is a profoundly significant development, which has so far been largely ignored. The media is full of articles about what Oswald Spengler one hundred years ago called 'The Decline of the West', and it seems as though every week there's another new book about the rise of the new Great Powers, but almost all of these books, articles and, of course, blogs deal with the political and economic consequences of this massive shift. The huge social and cultural implications have gone almost unremarked, although they've had a major impact on the way we live, and therefore inevitably on the world of brands and branding.

• • •

Western brands, or brands based around Western lifestyles from emerging markets, are now beginning to compete with brands from a completely different cultural background, and this development is hardly noticed, let alone discussed.

There are two sectors where Indian, Chinese and some other cultures have already had a massive impact on the way the world lives: eating and staying healthy. It's not going too far to say that in these two areas – food and fitness – there has been a highly successful cultural invasion, and the hegemony of the West has been challenged.

Western households look with equal interest, and absolutely no feelings of discrimination, at food from almost everywhere. Shall we have Indian, Italian, Spanish, Chinese or Brazilian this evening? Nothing unusual in squabbling over that kind of choice in the major cities of Europe and the United States. Supermarket shelves are stacked with Thai, Malaysian, Korean, Japanese and various other foods that were once thought exotic, and every High Street bursts with restaurants from all over the world.

In health, keeping fit, exercising, it's just the same. We are beginning to recognize acupuncture and other Chinese remedies, ayurveda and other Indian health practices, as entirely complementary to conventional Western products and workouts. Tai Chi, to coin a phrase, is now mainstream. So it's all happening.

What we have not yet got are brands that go with these products and services. There isn't one major global health and exercise brand from India – and there's no McDosa global Indian restaurant chain. Not yet. Within the next few decades it's clear to me that we will see Chinese and Indian branded medicines, and health products and services from other cultures, being sold over the counter in pharmacies all over the Western world, complementary to and competing with orthodox standard synthetic Western pharmaceutical products.

Being culturally, profoundly different and selling your brand around this difference demands self-confidence on a really global scale, an appropriate tone of voice and a heavy promotional mindset, and very few companies from emerging markets have got there yet. We are just on the verge of seeing it happen. There are a number of reasons why it has taken so long for brands like these to emerge. First, because Western brands created and understood mass markets early on. Second, because these brands became the admired model, so, almost inevitably, when organizations from growth markets wanted a bit of the action and tried to imitate them, their products looked like inferior copies. Third, because the techniques of mass marketing and branding were unfamiliar and these organizations didn't use them properly: they tried to win on price, not brand. And finally, and most importantly, the Western product had an in-built cultural superiority in the minds of consumers. Now that's all starting to change.

Today, our High Street is packed with Western brands, or what appear to be Western brands, although a lot of what's inside the packaging may actually be made in China, India, Vietnam or Thailand. Tomorrow, Chinese or Indian logos and designs will be on the outside of the package and, in many cases, what's inside will be different, too. The strengths of their brands will partly derive from their difference, but Chinese and Indian companies are only just beginning to understand how immense their opportunity is. Interestingly, Hermès, a major French luxury product company, has seen this trend and launched Shang Xia jointly with Jiang Qiong Er. Shang Xia is, says *The Financial Times*, *'that unusual thing in China: a brand that celebrates Chineseness rather than hiding it'*.[3] *'If it succeeds,'* the article goes on to say, *'it could herald the emergence of China as a power to reckon with in the global luxury business and provide a blueprint for other local brands to become globally competitive.'* Shang Xia, with its boutique in Shanghai and proposed outlets in Paris and Beijing, sells clothing, jewelry, furniture and objects all based around the image of an ancient Chinese civilization in which, says the *FT*, *'only the best would do'*.

In a later *Financial Times* 'How To Spend It' supplement, the journalist Lucia van der Post contributed an article called 'Beauty and the East', which is full of recommendations for Asian skin care products being marketed overseas. *'Asian brands are increasingly at the forefront of skin care in the West,'* she says.[4]

In this context the story of the Japanese automobile industry is instructive. In the 1970s the admired model was German, so if Japanese manufacturers wanted to build a car to compete in the luxury marketplace it had to feel and even look German. It was not considered marketing sense to use a Japanese brand name. So Toyota and Nissan – at the time manufacturers of cheapish Japanese cars – first began to challenge Western car-makers at the very top of the market by designing and building cars that looked and sounded like BMW and Mercedes-Benz. Naturally they tried to use Western brand names. Hence Lexus and Infiniti. In the event, both Lexus and Infiniti proved, over the longer term, to be superior in both quality and reliability to the German cars they emulated, so they gradually overcame prejudice and became very successful.

Japanese cars show a bit of confidence.

Look again. This isn't a Rolls-Royce. It's a Geely. 'It's a what?'

On to the next phase. Japanese luxury cars no longer have to pretend to be German to win. Sometimes they even claim direct superiority over German rivals. Now it's Korean cars that are going through a similar cycle, and just waiting in the wings are the Chinese car manufacturers. Rover, that collapsed and sad little rump of the once great British motor industry, is going through a Chinese reincarnation as Roewe. Various other Chinese manufacturers are still at the stage of marketing sophistication where they are shamelessly imitating any admired model they fancy, including Rolls-Royce. They are still very cautious about being seen to be Chinese, perhaps because they are not sufficiently self-confident, perhaps because their product quality is a bit inconsistent, and also perhaps because they don't quite 'get' branding.

Interestingly, though, the burgeoning Indian motor industry seems to be a bit different. Tata, India's most admired company and a leader in every industry you can think of, from steel to hotels to consumer products, is also big in the automotive world. Tata is India's largest producer of trucks and buses. In 2003, Tata's cheapest car was launched in Europe as the CityRover. It failed. In 2009, Tata introduced the Nano, a very cheap, economical car aimed at India's burgeoning middle class. The Nano doesn't pretend to be either European or Japanese: it doesn't emulate products from any other country. In fact, it hasn't even met EU safety standards. On the contrary, it quite clearly and self-confidently comes from India. It's certainly true that, as I write this, the Nano's record is mixed. Its distribution appears to be poor, it hasn't been selling well and it's unreliable. But it's new and these problems will presumably be dealt with. The intention is that it should be marketed around the world in a way which underlines its Indian provenance – cheap, reliable transport. That not only shows a lot of self-confidence, it also indicates the way the world is moving. Now Tata cars don't pretend to be European any more, except, of course, that Tata happens to own two major British brands which deliberately emphasize their Britishness – Jaguar and Land Rover.

There's something else happening, too, of which the Nano is the paradigm. Consumers in small towns and villages, and in poorer countries like Bangladesh, need simple devices to make life easier. They want them cheap and they want them reliable – things like water pumps, flushing lavatories, power from portable generators, and so on. Engineers and manufacturers in these countries are designing and manufacturing these kinds of products. It's called 'frugal technology'.

Godrej & Boyce have launched the ChotuKool, a battery-powered fridge for the poorer rural marketplace, and many such companies are finding a market for their products in the West as well. Mahindra & Mahindra are selling small tractors in Western markets. China's Haier makes a variety of cheap household products that work well and sell well in Western markets. A brilliant young Indian engineer designed, created, tested and implemented a small-scale sanitary napkin-making machine. It cost approximately £650, whereas the standard big company machine cost about £350,000. A self-help group from a village or small town can get together to buy the machine and create a workshop that employs up to 10 women and can make up to 120 napkins an hour. And it's highly successful. In 2013, it's estimated that only 5% of Indian woman can afford to use sanitary napkins. So there's plenty of room for growth ... and there are plenty of other examples.

Another market, then, is opening up of what you might call 'simplicity products'. These won't pretend to come from a Western background. On the contrary, their strength and positioning in the marketplace will derive from their emerging market origins. 'If we can make it for Indian small towns and villages, we can make it for you in Nigeria – or for your trailer or second home in the United States.'

So where is it all going to end? Over the next generation or two some people will smell of Chinese scents, anoint themselves with Korean creams, furnish their homes with Indian branded textiles, go to sleep on Brazilian branded beds, wear Thai branded clothes and exercise in Asian branded activities of various kinds. Consumers all over the world who are already burdened by a plethora of choice are going to have even more to cope with. The first half of the 21st century will see a mass of new brands from what we now call emerging markets, and these will be underlining and emphasizing their unique national heritage in the global marketplace. Just you wait and see.

That doesn't mean that rich Chinese and Indians and Brazilians will stop buying Bentley and Breitling and Burberry. What it does mean is that the West will fall in love with all kinds of products – luxury products, frugal technology products – all over again, just like it did a few hundred years ago.

7

National Prosperity and Nation Branding.

Branding the nation came into fashion with the Age of
Enlightenment. The slogans, or straplines, or vision statements,
as some people might now call them – 'Life, Liberty and
the Pursuit of Happiness' and 'Liberté, Égalité, Fraternité',
respectively of revolutionary United States and newly republican
France – set the style of nation building for the whole of the
19th century, when the modern nation emerged fully formed
as an ideological construct. The nation was, and is, proclaimed
by and symbolized in its own highly coloured mythology –
heroes celebrated in arts, music, literature, sport and, above
all, in stories of war, in battles lost and won. The nation state
bathed itself in its own self-generating nostalgia and a vast
pile of emotional baggage, which provided an overwhelmingly

powerful sense of belonging for its citizens. Britain's Diamond Jubilee celebration of 2012, when the nation appeared to be intoxicated by its own stability, longevity and unique charm, all symbolized by its reigning monarch, was perhaps its 21st-century apotheosis.

During the 19th century the mythic power of the nation state became so overwhelming that it dominated the political destiny and shape of Europe. France was the first big modern European nation state; Italy and Germany followed. In Italy, despite the fact that most people living in the peninsula couldn't speak the national language, never travelled around the country and had no conception of the nation as a whole, the drive from idealists like Mazzini, political intriguers like Cavour and popular military heroes like Garibaldi, eventually became irresistible. Immensely influential cultural figures, like Giuseppe Verdi, added even more glamour, excitement, romance and nationalist fervour to the mix. The national brand became so powerful that its ideology was unstoppable. The Risorgimento brought a united Italy.

Throughout the 20th century the momentum to form nation states was apparently irreversible. The Habsburg, Romanov and Ottoman multinational empires collapsed during and after World War I. The British, French, Dutch, Portuguese and Belgian empires fell apart after World War II. Then in 1989 the Soviet empire disintegrated. Each time a huge tidal wave of new or revived nation states emerged, every one with its own collection of flags, uniforms, anthems and all the rest of it. It usually embraced a national airline just to wave the flag around a bit.

In 1919, there were 42 members of the League of Nations. In 1945, when the United Nations was formed, it had 51 members. Today, in 2013, the United Nations has 193 members. Over the past two centuries the idea of the nation state has become so dominant that it's virtually impossible to conceive of a world organized in any other way.

Although no one has been quite able to define what the nation is, we all recognize it when we see it and it exercises an extraordinarily powerful pull over the imaginations of peoples everywhere. Eric Hobsbawm, one of the great historians of nationalism, puts it this way: *'Language, religion, territory, history, sport, culture and the rest of it make up national sentiment.... National sentiment makes the nation.'*[1]

The main thrust of 19th- and 20th-century national identity was domestic – to create and sustain internal cohesion and pride. Economic and commercial issues were important, but secondary. The external dimension was about influencing, and often dominating, neighbours and reaching out to the national diaspora. The near neighbour was, and often still is, the enemy, 'The Other'.

There just doesn't seem to be any alternative governance system. When multinational empires disappeared during the 20th century, nothing quite replaced them. The European Union is currently faltering and rudderless; the United Nations (the nearest we have to a world administrative governing or mediating body) is made up of nation states which use it as a platform to squabble with each other. New nation states are continually popping up, and wars – minor wars, ethnic clashes, civil wars, religious wars – both between nations and inside nations, proliferate.

And still new nations keep on emerging. In Africa, South Sudan acquired national status in the second decade of the 21st century; in Europe, Belgium might well split into Flanders and

Wallonia; the Catalans and Basques want 'freedom from Spain'; in Britain, Scotland is dominated by the Scottish National Party, which eventually looks for some kind of independent status. One might reasonably ask, in the case of the European aspirants anyway: independence from what, from whom and for what? They just want it, that's all. 'We want it because we want it. That's why we want it.' It is absolutely and overwhelmingly visceral.

• • •

But over the past fifty years or so something has happened, a massive change that, in principle at any rate, has altered everything. It's called 'globalization'. Of course, in the fifty or so year period before World War I, there was globalization, too, but not on the scale that we see today. Just as the new nation states led by France and the United States challenged and changed the meaning of nationality in the late 18th century, so globalization is doing the same in the 21st century.

Roger Cohen, writing in the *New York Times*, put it very neatly: '*The nation state seems as riveting as in the 19th century, an obstinate ideal that pulls at primal heartstrings and mocks logic.*'[2] He goes on to say, '*Globalization is a contradiction of everything the nation state stands for.*' And in a sense, of course, he's right.

There are no frontiers now, especially for corporations. The world is just one place and you can pick and choose where you do things, regardless of national borders. Anything can be made anywhere. For example, aircraft, or bits of aircraft, can be made in fifty different places and put together somewhere else quite different. Research and development can be carried out simultaneously in four or five countries, outsourcing in a few more. It's not only corporations: almost everyone is influenced by globalization. The movement of people – as tourists, as immigrants, as temporary workers, even as terrorists – operates on a scale never even approached before. Ordinary people take two or three holidays a year in places that were once thought of as remote and exotic. And massive investments made by rich states like Qatar – sovereign investment funds into the infrastructure of countries all over the world – accelerate the trend in which nobody really knows who owns what, and where everything, everywhere, may be owned by somebody else ... and usually is.

On top of all that, social media – blogs, Twitter and the rest of it – have transformed the way the world works and lives. Anybody can get in touch with anyone else at any time ... and does. Of course, there's lots of interference from authoritarian regimes but, as we have seen so often, it doesn't always work.

• • •

In theory, then, national borders hardly count, at least in many spheres of activity. But, if borders are so porous and globalization is taking over, surely the national brand should be in sharp decline? The new world order should mean the end of the nation state as we know it. But that's not happening. So why are more and more nations involved in national branding programmes? What is happening?

Paradoxically, perhaps, globalization has not killed off the concept of the nation state. On the contrary, it makes nations and national identity even more compelling, because now the national brand and, within the nation, the city brand

and, sometimes, across nations, the regional brand, have a statistically measurable economic aim, as well as a traditional, emotional, ideological purpose.

That is what lies behind the idea of the nation as a brand. Branding the nation has become vital for economic success. It's simple – at least, in principle: popular and well-liked nations attract more tourists and more investment and can charge more for their exports than little-liked or little-known nations. And the competition between nations is intense. The more globalization, the more competition.

And that increasingly is why nations are still struggling to brand themselves. There's a commercial imperative. They don't so much want to make war with their neighbours as to become richer than them. If you want to be prosperous as a nation state, you had better start branding yourself. As the writer Philip Bobbitt puts it: nation states are becoming market states and they are not finding it easy. In fact, they are finding it very hard. Mostly they make a mess of it. They don't know what to say. They don't know how to say it. They don't know who to say it to.

National identity is now increasingly concerned with competing with your neighbours to attract more economic activity than they do. Globalization has modified both the purpose and the nature of national branding. These are the three measurable areas in which competition takes place: tourism, investment and export. And there's another – reputation – which is much more elusive.

We all love to associate products with places, which, incidentally, may be the reason why so many of those gruesome 'I love London/NY/Mumbai/Belfast' T-shirts still litter the streets. It was fine when Milton Glaser created it for New York. But now look!

Different places have different specialist skills, which, in some way, seem to encapsulate their particular personality and style. America, Britain, France, Germany, Italy, Spain, Japan and a few other countries have this. They can charge more for what they export because people value it more. Other nations such as Lithuania, Slovenia and Paraguay, and even Turkey, Mexico or South Korea, don't have the same cachet.

If the nation doesn't market itself aggressively, if it doesn't get investment, if it doesn't attract tourists and it can't sell what it makes at a high enough price, it will stay poorer than its neighbour. If a nation wants more prosperity, it has to fight to make its identity more valuable and more attractive.

Let's just look at the three broad categories in a bit of detail – tourism, foreign direct investment and export. On the face of it, all of these activities may be perceived as separate from each other. They may appear to have different audiences or target markets and there doesn't seem to be much overlap between them, but, in reality, they are mutually supportive and, collectively, they add to national influence – what is sometimes called 'soft power'.

1. Tourism

This is usually managed by a national tourist office or tourist board. Promotions, especially for hot countries, are mostly about sun, sea and sand, and the advertising campaigns from the majority of these countries are bland, banal and interchangeable. But tourism can be about so much more than sun, sea and package tours. It can be about food, or architecture and culture, or adventure holidays – or all of these. It might even lead to the purchase of a holiday home (or is that foreign

direct investment)? Tourism can be a path to bigger investment of a quite different sort. You like the place, the climate is good, they speak your language, the schools seem to be excellent, the tax rates and other incentives seem competitive, your personal experience influences you. OK, that may be a bit far-fetched, but who knows? You might get some colleagues from your company to take a look, commission a study, ultimately even persuade your company to set up its research and development activity here. The point is that tourism promotion, if it's to work effectively, is an intrinsic part of the way the whole country markets itself. Everything must be mutually supportive.

What's the difference?

2. Foreign Direct Investment

Every nation has an FDI activity. Nations compete with each other, at least in theory, to make investment opportunities attractive: tax breaks, no red tape, easy employment regulations, a highly qualified workforce that speaks your language, good infrastructure, and so on. The traditional assumption is that investment is manufacture, but it can also mean research and development, industrial and commercial real estate, banking, insurance, retail, exploration and development of natural resources, call centres and other forms of outsourcing. In fact, it can be almost anything that involves putting money, people and other resources into a country. This is an opportunity for the region and the city as much as for the nation. Look at London. Well, we will in the next chapter.

3. Export

This doesn't just mean products. It can mean people, anyone from academics to plumbers to labourers on building sites. Kerala, a state in southern India, derives a significant proportion of its income from export of people: funds are regularly repatriated from those of its citizens who work in the Gulf States. Export can mean finished products, but it can also mean raw materials for processing. Kazakhstan has suddenly become oil-rich. And it looks as though Mongolia will become even richer through its mineral resources. In fact, export can mean pretty much anything or anybody the nation sends abroad.

But, for many countries, export means brand export – literally, the export of its brands, quite often consumer brands. And these brands can have a profound impact on the way the nation is perceived. Take Italy and fashion. If it's 'Made in Italy' you can charge more for it. Not only that: Armani, Gucci, Prada and the rest of them add glamour and excitement to the idea of Italy as a whole.

They, and all the other Italian fashion houses, are not entirely phoney but they play and pander to a deep, romantic, irrational feeling buried inside almost all of us to want something that comes from somewhere special – even if we suspect it doesn't. Major consumer brands from Prada in Italy to Coca-Cola in

Worldwide, Peroni equals Italy.

the United States to Guinness in Ireland don't just sell the product, they sell the nation they come from. Look at any Irish bar anywhere in the world. For many of the world's citizens, Guinness is Ireland.

• • •

As I have pointed out elsewhere, in some cases, if you know the brand, you can make assumptions about the country. McDonald's, Disney and Coca-Cola define one idea of the United States; Apple, Intel, Microsoft define another. But both are the United States. Mercedes, BMW and Audi are Germany – engineering precision. These brands have a massive halo effect on their country of origin. Other brands in the same sector can grow and flourish.

If you happen to be a country like France, Italy or Britain, country of origin is associated with particular types of products, and inevitably also with national prestige and therefore a higher price tag. On the other hand, if you come from Latvia or maybe even Poland, it doesn't work like that. Dr. Irena Eris, an excellent, well-packaged Polish cosmetic brand, makes little headway in export markets. Who wants Polish cosmetics when you can buy French, even if the Polish stuff is much cheaper? Maybe even because it's much cheaper. It's no good saying Helena Rubinstein came from Poland: that was a long time ago.

Neutrogena, a company owned by Johnson & Johnson and registered in California, has fantasized a relationship with Norway and the Arctic seas where sturdy fisherfolk, whose hands are chapped and cut by ropes and clean cold air, soothe their distressed extremities with a natural product that is, in

Neutrogena: a Norwegian fantasy, made in the USA.

fact, made in synthetic form by Neutrogena in New Jersey. But hence the dinky little Norwegian flag on some Neutrogena products.

Just occasionally, the brand is better known than the nation it comes from and that doesn't give the nation the lift-off it needs, like Samsung and South Korea. In other situations, the country that makes the brand is just the manufacturer – that's all. Slovakia makes lots of cars but I've never seen 'Made in Slovakia' on a Citroën or a Toyota. Why? Because Citroën is seen to be French and Toyota Japanese and 'Made in Slovakia' adds nothing. Even if it comes off production lines in Bratislava, it could just as well be 'Made in China'. Nor have I seen 'Made in Romania' on a Dacia, the Renault subsidiary.

In fact, as I pointed out in Chapter 6, most of the world's nations are just beginning to come to grips with the issue of brands. It will take time, expertise, patience and money – all in short supply – to get it right.

• • •

Meanwhile, there are a number of rating agencies that purport to rank the popularity and success of one nation compared with another. Rich nations that are seen to behave well and have a good humanitarian record have a higher place in the pecking order than poor, self-destructive nations, which are seen as corrupt and lawless. Unsurprisingly then, Norway always ranks high, Pakistan always ranks low. In detail, of course, it's a lot more complex than that. Infrastructure, honesty, efficiency, education, the arts, sports, and so on are all weighed with and against each other in order to create a rating in the pecking order.

Well-known nations attract much more attention than unknown nations. The United States is better known to more people than Paraguay. The BRICS – those emerging nations with emerging economies – are increasingly influential and responding well to opportunities. The old, formerly powerful but still influential nations – I call them Legacy Nations: Britain, France, Germany, Italy, Spain, and so on – also have a secure place in people's minds more or less all over the world. The brands they export both sustain and are sustained by their country of origin.

But this new situation in which nations compete with each other commercially to attract investment and tourism and to export their products and services also creates new kinds of opportunities. Niches open up. Some cities, like London or Shanghai, or regions, like Silicon Valley, have a reputation that's distinct from their national base. In addition, city states like Dubai and Singapore are becoming regional transport or financial hubs, or both.

But while some nations and cities see a gap and seize opportunities to develop and exploit their profile, many others – indeed, most of the nations and regions and cities of the world – are reactive. They don't do much to make themselves known or liked. They remain little known except to their immediate neighbours, unless some hideous disaster or terrorist incident or nasty civil war breaks out, at which point, for a few days or weeks, they become headline news – bad headline news – before disappearing from sight once again. And this doesn't help their national brand much. That is one reason why Kosovo, for example, struggles to attract investment.

Even peaceful and relatively prosperous nations remain barely known in the world at large. How many times are the

Slovenian and Slovakian flags. Slovenia is the one at the top, I think.

Baltics confused with the Balkans? How often is Slovenia confused with Slovakia? In this case, just to compound the confusion further, the two countries even have similar flags.

Sometimes a few little nations may think of clubbing together to promote themselves collectively – like, say, the Nordic region or, maybe, the Alpine region – but then they often compete internally, too. It's all a bit tentative and new and more than a bit confused.

The reality is that, despite all the ratings and the rankings and the apparently objective analyses, most people in most nations are ignorant of and indifferent to other nations in the rest of the world. So, while every nation in the world – the big ones, the small ones, the old ones, the new ones – is competing with every other for investment, tourism and export, and the new city states, the regions, almost every other place you can think of, are joining the race, most places are either not seen at all or are perceived through a fog of myth, anecdote and grossly exaggerated stereotypes. We just don't know much about each other.

Even Britain, still quite a large and important nation (just), is, in my personal experience, seen as a mix of the Queen, Buckingham Palace, Sherlock Holmes, bad food, bad weather and the Beatles – or, sometimes, the Rolling Stones. Not much Damien Hirst there. While Britain ranks high for tertiary education and, broadly speaking, decent behaviour on the global scene, and London ranks high for finance, academia and culture, the anecdotal and simplistic history and the isolated incidents have, somehow or other, morphed into a distorted but deeply held series of perceptions which are, for many people in the world, their reality.

British stereotypes sold to tourists in Liberty, London (opposite): Made in Germany's idea of London.

So what chance does a smallish, newish nation have of launching itself as a destination for tourism or outsourcing or research and development? Sometimes a little nation can get a lucky break, like Montenegro with the James Bond film *Casino Royale*. But not often. A few nations, mainly but not exclusively Nordic, have built a reputation over generations for decent, humanitarian behaviour, but sometimes even this frays around the edges.

Of course, a nation can build or re-build a reputation, but it takes time, money, organization, a clear sense of direction – that is, deciding whom you want to influence – and an understanding of what makes the nation unique. And it has to be led. And the leadership has to come from government.

National branding is harder than it used to be. The old-style national branding programmes, with their flags, uniforms, ceremonies, anthems, sporting and cultural events, and ritualistic celebrations of national victories, were essentially aimed at domestic audiences. They were inspirational and they appealed to national loyalties. National anthems were stuffed to the brim with sonorous platitudes about the glories of the nation, unique in its gift to the world. Primary and secondary education and compulsory military service also played a large part in creating and sustaining national myths for the internal, domestic audience, which now play a subordinate role.

The newer national branding programmes are primarily aimed at external audiences who will usually only have a superficial and ill-informed view of other countries and who are swayed by emotion, by myth, by rumour, by sporting or cultural success, by big brands that come from somewhere.

The branding issues are complex, interrelated and have a long-term life span, while governments – particularly in democracies – are, for the most part, short-term, tactical and opportunistic. Their different ministries and departments are isolated and mutually suspicious. They guard their fiefdom jealously. Most governments are very bad at understanding the implications of a national branding programme and worse at initiating and sustaining it over time. Government – the public sector – simply cannot do it by itself. It needs partners.

If a national branding programme is going to work, it demands, in addition to a long-term vision, collaboration between public sector and private sector, a meeting ground between people from the arts, sport, industry, finance, commerce and education and other significant sectors, and it must also gain the sympathy and understanding of the domestic audience, so the media are extremely important.

There are other issues, too. Who is in charge of the programme? The Prime Minister? The Economics Minister? Some other minister, or group of ministers? Should there be a symbolic leader – the President, the King or Queen? Who funds it? How much should you spend? For how long? What should you spend it on? What is the role of the private sector? How do you know if it's working?

I've tried discussing these issues with governments all over the world. Everybody agrees in principle that tourism, direct investment and export have to be co-ordinated, long-term and linked with softer issues such as sport, culture, the arts and everything else, and that tactical short-term advertising campaigns should be part of a long-term programme. But in practice, for the most part, they can't make it work. It's all too competitive and unco-ordinated. No organization is set up to manage it, or if it is it soon collapses. National branding isn't seen as a coherent entity. Foreign policy, soft power, economic and industrial policy, tourism policy, supporting and working with the private sector are all treated as separate silos or fiefdoms, each with its own complex, self-regarding bureaucracy and budget. Sport and culture are separate again, and so nothing hangs together: nothing supports anything else, except by accident.

Nor have governments, for the most part, thought through how to influence their own electorate to understand the purpose of a national branding programme or to create a situation in which voters are engaged in and support the development of such a programme. To take an example, near home for me, the British public have no conception of the global influence of the BBC as a cultural tool for the objectivity and impartiality of Britain. Within Britain the BBC is seen as just another broadcaster: big, influential, bossy, sometimes maybe a bit self-important and prone to trip over itself. There's absolutely no domestic understanding of the immense influence the BBC has as a decent and honourable voice for Britain worldwide. Domestically, the BBC is much more the subject of criticism than the object of praise. Globally the reverse is true. The BBC is seen in the world to speak for a respected Britain. The British themselves don't, for the most part, know this and, maybe, if they knew, they wouldn't care.

This is why, so very often, where branding – the nation, the city or the region – is successful, it's because of accident or individual endeavour through serendipity, rather than comprehensive and coherent, effective planning.

· · ·

The example of Spain is significant. For three hundred years Spain was in decline. Since 1975 its renaissance has been remarkable. The reality has changed dramatically in the last fifty years, from a poverty-stricken dictatorship in Europe's far south to an influential, medium-sized nation, and perceptions have changed in tune with this.

Clothes designer Adolfo Dominguez, film-maker Pedro Almodovar, architect and engineer Santiago Calatrava, tennis superstar Rafael Nadal, Formula One champion Fernando Alonso and the European and World Champion Spanish soccer teams are not government hacks hired by the hour. They are world-class figures, whose work shares the courage and optimism of the new Spain. Partly, at any rate, because over many years the Spanish government in the centre and the regions has worked hard at creating and projecting a courageous and optimistic vision, based on a reality of change, which inspired them and in which they shared. Spanish fashion brands like Zara, financial institutions like Santander and major business organizations like Ferrovial have all contributed to, shared and benefited from this vision.

It's certainly true, as I write this, that Spain is going through a rough time and that its economy is weak, that the regions didn't control their budgets, that the *cajas*, the regional banks, were badly managed and in some cases corrupt, that the property boom was uncontrolled, and so on, and that at least for the time being Spain can help serve as an example of how to get it wrong rather than the other way round. But quite a few nations, including the United States and much of the European Union, have had their share of problems, too. And Spain can and will recover. It is now, for the first time in centuries, an intrinsic part of modern Europe. It has a national brand that's important for Europe. As Spain's finances recover, it will have to revitalize and re-present its national brand. It's just one rather dramatic example of a nation which, for the sake of its own continuing prosperity, has to promote that national brand. And the idea of Spain can be encapsulated in one word – 'passion' – and this gives the Spanish national brand a huge potential advantage. Whether Spain will be able to organize itself to exploit this situation is, of course, an entirely different matter.

• • •

All countries communicate all the time. They send out millions of messages every day, through political action or inaction, through popular culture, through products, services, food, film, arts, sport, humanitarian behaviour, soft power ... everything. Regions and cities promote themselves. Branded products have 'Made in X' scrawled all over them. Collectively, all these millions of messages represent an idea of what the nation as a whole is up to, what it feels, what it wants, what it believes in, what it's like. It should be the task of government – with a very light touch – to set the tone for these messages and to lead by example, where appropriate, so that a picture which is credible, realistic, individual and true can emerge.

Governments can create the mood and lead and co-ordinate the new image. Coherent efforts within every department – culture, arts, sport, industry, education, transport and environment and, of course, foreign affairs – can stimulate, inspire and steer. There has to be a powerful visual focus, an agreement to make it work, and an adequate power base and funding.

The idea behind the programme should be to align perceptions with reality, so that the nation is seen for what it is now and what it is becoming, not for what it was twenty or fifty years ago.

So how can you get it right? The key is to get a clear core idea for the nation which is differentiated and true, make it manifest by visualizing it and implementing it on all those on-going activities where it's possible and credible and, in this way, to create or co-ordinate a movement that influential organizations and individuals outside government circles join, because it suits them, because it helps them. Then you get a movement which is self-sustaining.

A few years ago I outlined the basic steps in national brand building. I think it might be worthwhile expanding on them:

- Set up a working party with representatives of government, industry, the arts, education, sport, the media, and so on, to start the programme: a public/private relationship.
- Determine who are the most important target audiences externally, both in terms of nation and sector.
- Carry out quantitative and qualitative research to see how the nation is perceived, both by its own people and by target nations abroad. It's a great mistake to assume that outsiders know very much, or anything at all for that matter, about your own country. I was once shown a map of Europe by a Taiwanese official in which there was no British Isles.
- Develop a process of consultation with opinion-leaders to look at national strengths and weaknesses and compare them with the results of the internal and external studies.
- Create the central idea on which the strategy is based with professional advisors. It needs to be a powerful, simple idea

that captures the unique qualities of the nation and can be used as a base from which the entire programme can be developed so that perceptions can be aligned with reality. Yes, we know that every nation claims that it's welcoming, friendly, industrious and charming, but Japan isn't Britain, Germany isn't Brazil and Lithuania isn't Colombia. So find the difference and emphasize it.

- Develop ways of articulating the central idea visually. Designers should not just look at logos and tourist advertising but at everything, from the design of airports where visitors arrive to the embassies that represent the nation abroad.
- Look at how the messages required for tourism, inward investment and export can be co-ordinated and modulated so that they are appropriate for each audience but remain mutually supportive.
- Create a liaison system through the working party to launch and sustain the programme in government activities and to encourage supportive action from appropriate organizations in commerce, industry, the arts, media, and so on.
- Carry out research on a regular basis in target markets to monitor changing perceptions.

The project should then be rolled out gradually, without making a big song and dance. This means looking at every opportunity – not just the obvious trade fairs, advertising and commercial work in embassies, but the reception that people get in airports, stations, government buildings, broadcasting, restaurants; everywhere, in fact, that can contribute to the idea of a country. It's worth remembering that people are influenced by things they see, feel and eat as much as by what they read or hear. That's why film festivals are quite as significant as commercial missions. Find the significant touch points and emphasize them.

And remember, whenever a campaign is launched which has a tactical short-term purpose, it should be seen to be linked to the whole. Increasingly, so-called place branding is becoming associated with campaigns: campaigns to increase out-of-season tourism or, for example, campaigns to promote local cheese or local crafts. All fine, but they must be linked to the long-term programme. A programme to promote a nation can be associated with any number of short-term campaigns provided that these campaigns fulfil the criteria of the overall programme and that they are linked to give coherence to and derive coherence from the whole.

A successful brand will be seen as a key national asset. Increasingly, no country will be able to ignore the way the rest of the world sees it. Politicians everywhere now realize that every nation has an identity. They can either seek to manage this, or it will manage them.

There is, however, one important caveat. A nation-branding programme in a democratic country is based around the co-operation of the willing in a long-term project to improve perceptions of the nation and increase and further prosperity. Such a programme must be sustained over a long period of time, regardless of which political party is in power. It is only in an authoritarian state that the national branding programme becomes a political propaganda machine deliberately devised to sustain the regime. There have been, and there still are, plenty of those around. Avoid them.

8

Branding the Place.

The country we now call Turkey has changed its name and its identity so many times you can't even begin to count. The Turkish landmass has been part of the mythology and history of Europe, Central Asia and the Middle East ever since anyone can remember or write it down.

The Greeks fought the Trojans in what is now called Turkey. The ruins of many great Greek city states like Ephesus, uncovered by archaeologists in the 19th century, are now Turkish tourist attractions, picked over by elderly Germans and Brits with a guidebook in one hand and a walking stick in the other. They are part of what some people visit Turkey for.

Ancient Greece – of which much of present-day Turkey was once a part – was then absorbed into the Roman Empire and the Romans made themselves so comfortable there that, as the Western part of the empire declined, they eventually transferred their capital to Byzantium, later renamed after the first Christian Roman emperor, Constantine. Today we call it Istanbul.

The Eastern Roman Empire or, if you like, the Byzantine Empire, which lasted about a thousand years and was the successor to Rome, was a highly sophisticated, extremely complex and deviously self-destructive political, cultural, economic and religious entity – hence the current implications of the word 'byzantine'. The Byzantines constructed some of modern Turkey's greatest and most admired buildings and left some of its most astonishing architectural legacies. The Hagia Sophia (until relatively recently a mosque) in Istanbul was built by the Byzantines as the Cathedral of Santa Sophia, home of the Eastern Orthodox Church.

A thousand years is a long time and, in the end, the Byzantine Empire, having been threatened with destruction by almost everyone you can think of, including its major competitors in the practice of Christianity, the Catholic Crusaders, who virtually destroyed Constantinople in 1204, finally fell in 1453 to the Ottoman Turkish dynasty. It was they who changed the name of the capital city from Constantinople to Istanbul.

So that brings us, a bit breathlessly, to what began sometimes to be called Turkey, and to another major change of dynasty, direction and what we might now call brand. The Ottomans were Muslim – Central Asian in origin, language, dress and style – and they were different. Over a very short time, the Turks conquered half of Europe, and they terrified and fascinated the remaining half for about two hundred years. They were the ultimate 'Other' and they were right outside the Western

European door: in fact, at times it looked as though they were pushing inside. The Ottomans were only stopped at the gates of Vienna in 1683. After that it was the usual slow decline, the affliction of all empires. But perceptions of Turkey, even today in the 21st century, are influenced by the impact that the Ottomans made on Europe from the 15th to the early 20th century.

For a time, Ottoman Turkey was apparently irresistible, and there was a genuine fear that the Western European Christian world would be overwhelmed by these people alien in religion, language, customs and culture. This visceral fear of 'the Terrible Turk' has lingered on in West European folk memory to this day.

The reality of Ottoman Turkey was, in many ways, different from its image in Western Europe as ferocious and violent. Ottoman Turkey was not a nation in the modern sense. The Ottoman Empire was multinational, multilingual and, for much of the time, rather tolerant in an odd sort of way – certainly considerably more tolerant than much of Christian Europe. There were plenty of Armenians, Greeks and other Christian minorities in the Ottoman Empire. Venetians, Genoese, French, English, all set up shop in Istanbul, many of them very successfully. Sephardi Jews, thrown out of Catholic Spain, found a home in the Muslim Ottoman Empire. At its height the empire was vast, stretching from the borders of Persia to (for quite some time) the middle of Europe, and it dominated the Balkans and the Eastern Mediterranean until, like every other empire, bits of it just crumbled off. But perceptions of Turkey as cruel, ruthless and threatening persisted.

In 1914, at the start of World War I, a disintegrating Turkey made a big mistake and joined the side that lost – Germany and its allies. By 1919 what little was left of the Ottomans was

finished. The empire disappeared; so did the Ottoman dynasty.
A republic was proclaimed and another Turkey emerged. This
time, however, the rebranding programme was not casual,
incidental or even accidental; it was profound, thought-through,
initiated and executed thoroughly, ruthlessly and remarkably
speedily by Mustafa Kemal, the hero of Gallipoli, who set an
example in the rebranding effort by changing his name to
Atatürk, father of the Turks. Atatürk completely, deliberately, and
in an almost reckless rush, reinvented Turkey. His programme
was arguably the most complete rebranding operation any
nation has ever gone through and stayed with over time.

Atatürk was, of course, an authoritarian. He created a unitary
monolingual nation state out of a multinational, multilingual,
sprawling empire. In 1923, he declared a republic. Polygamy
was abolished. The fez was banned. A Latinized alphabet was
adopted. Civil marriage was introduced and family names became
mandatory. What we now call 'ethnic cleansing', especially between
Greeks and Turks, took place on a massive scale. And that was just
for starters. Behind a fairly thin, almost transparent veil, there
was the authoritarian military presence to keep things secular.

And that's the way things stayed in Turkey between the two
world wars. Turkey played no role in World War II, except as a
place where spies tried to find out what the other side was doing.

After the war, Western Europe grew very fast and it needed
labour. Turks from the Anatolian plains, the villages and
small towns provided it. Rugged-looking men, their wives in
headscarves, with lots of children, came into Western Europe in
the 1960s and '70s, and even as late as the '80s, as 'guest workers'
(*Gastarbeiter*). Putting it less politely, that meant they could be sent
back where they came from when they were not needed anymore.

*Rebranding Turkey: Atatürk
introducing the Roman alphabet,
1928.*

They arrived in their thousands, in their hundreds of thousands, especially to West Germany, as it then was. They also influenced perceptions of Turkey, adding something perhaps to the historical view of Turkey as alien and a bit wild. A movie called *Midnight Express* about life in a Turkish prison didn't help either.

Then Turkey began to develop its southern coast as a holiday destination, competing with Spain and other Southern European and Mediterranean coastlines. Hundreds of thousands of visitors from Northern Europe found a new, charming Turkey with wonderful food, delightful people and an astonishing amount of history and legend to gawp at. Sailing on the Turkish coast became great fun for up-market holiday-makers (I love it).

Next, after quite a few years of inflation and directionless, unstable government, Turkish political life settled down and Turkey began to industrialize and grow. Around the turn of the 21st century, it started to get richer. It is, as I write this, growing at the same rate, more or less, as Brazil, China and India, and is going through the same phases of development. There are a few large family businesses involved in a wide range of activities, from manufacturing to finance to digital technology. There's also a growing sector in manufacturing components and finished products, much of which are sold on to major Western European and American companies, who put their own brand names on. And Turkey also has a big consumer products industry.

Turkey is, of course, on Europe's doorstep; a bit of it is actually inside Europe. It has been an applicant, of a kind, for membership of the EU since the 1970s. For all sorts of reasons, mostly unpleasant and unspoken, most EU countries want to keep it out. They don't say so, but they don't want poor Muslims inside and they still have the folk memory of the Terrible Turk.

But now that Turkey is getting richer and stronger, and the EU is getting poorer and weaker, maybe it will be a bit different. Turkey now has real political clout and is using it. It's a mildly Islamist, non-Arab state. It has real influence in its home territories of Central Asia and the Middle East, as well as in Southeastern Europe (the Balkans). Domestically, as I write this, it seems as though there may be further political turmoil, so things may not stay quite so calm. However, on the plus side, Istanbul is one of the world's most beautiful, interesting and vibrant cities, and spends a great deal of money, time, energy and charm hosting one international event after another, whether in design, music, art or architecture. In 2010, it was European City of Culture. Put that together with the Mediterranean coast as an attractive holiday location, and contemporary Turkey has a lot to say about itself.

The profound mismatch between static, outdated perceptions and a rapidly changing and fascinating reality is always a source of misunderstanding, damage and lost opportunity. Perceptions of Turkey in the world, especially in Europe, need to be aligned with the reality of Turkey today – a dynamic, attractive powerhouse.

It's not that nobody knows Turkey. On the contrary, Turkey is very well known globally. But impressions of the country are muddled and confused. A mixture of ancient Christian antagonism going back some six hundred years, of a poor Muslim country, of *Gastarbeiter*, of a modern vibrant and fast-growing society, of an increasingly independent and influential political entity we ought to keep on good terms with, and, perhaps above all, of another rapidly growing economy right on

Europe's doorstep, though now further confused by domestic discontent: all these perceptions are muddled up together.

The action has to come from Turkey. There are plenty of brilliant independent initiatives, both public and private, but there's no overall strategic thrust; no clear long-term idea. In tourism, foreign direct investment and political influence, Turkey is making a mark but it's all incoherent. And there are major weaknesses to overcome, too.

Turkey needs major brands which create a halo for Turkish products and services worldwide and which underline Turkey's significant and individual position in the world. Right now, whichever way you look at it and wherever you look – from fashion to olive oil, food, wine, components, white goods and electronics – a product with the label 'Made in Turkey' would imply cheap, clumsy and probably charmless and badly designed. But Turkey has some world-class products which could do with world-class promotion so that 'Made in Turkey' seems worth spending money on.

Turkey is the most dramatic example I can think of that has everything an emerging, influential nation could possibly need: size, geographical position, leading technology, political influence, physical beauty, culture, art, food, sport, history, soft power – the lot. And now it needs to launch a coherent national brand programme, led by the public sector with involvement from all areas of the private sector, to re-emerge as the significant influence it once was in an entirely different context. It needs to align perception with reality.

• • •

Turkey is a monolingual state descended from a multilingual, multicultural empire. Before the nation overwhelmed and replaced them, there were plenty of governance systems like that in the world. Multilingual, multinational empires, like the Holy Roman Empire, lived for centuries side by side with all kinds of other entities – states ruled by the Pope, by dukes, by bishops, by princes of various kinds – all inhabited by people whose loyalty and affiliation was to the town they lived in, or more often the village. The concept of nationality meant nothing to them. Joseph Roth's novel, *The Radetzky March*, written in 1932, about the last years of the Austro-Hungarian Empire, examines the mutual incompatibility, almost incomprehension, of each point of view.

Then there was the city state. Ancient Greece was based around city states; so was much of medieval and Renaissance Europe. In the Middle Ages the Hanseatic League was a formidable combination of trading city states dotted around Northern Europe. Fragmented memories of it still linger on here and there (curiously, the automobile number plate system in Germany still uses the initial 'H' for Hansestadt and HL, HB, HH are initials of Hansestadt Lübeck, Hansestadt Bremen and Hansestadt Hamburg). In the end, though, none of these entities could resist the rise of the nation state. All the city states, the Hanseatic League, Florence of the Medicis, Milan of the Sforzas, even Venice, the greatest of them all, disappeared (Napoleon put the finishing touches to Venice, by then a shadow of itself, right at the beginning of the 19th century).

With the emergence of the modern nation state, the city state seemed quite dead. Now, two hundred years later, it's back, and a few are highly successful. Some are entrepots, which have seized the opportunities thrown up by globalization. They live on trade and on movement of people and products, and sometimes on tourism. They don't make much; they mostly buy and sell and invest. They have an immense global impact and a very high profile. Dubai and Singapore are two outstanding examples. With small populations, they are much better known globally and much more influential than many much larger countries, let alone cities. Romania and Hungary, for example, and other Central European countries, have populations two or three times the size but they don't have the global influence and the profile of these city states. Broadly speaking, images of these city states are positive. They don't sell many products; they sell themselves.

Without heavy, positive and continuous self-promotion, they couldn't exist. Both Dubai and Singapore have massive airports. They are hubs for both passengers and freight. In a sense, they are the aerotropolis, already realized.

Singapore is, for me, particularly interesting. Unlike Turkey, it's new. In the early 19th century it was a swamp at the far end of Malaya. The British had just, with great reluctance, returned the East Indies to the Dutch and were looking for another naval base. A British colonial civil servant, Stamford Raffles, found the strategic spot and developed it. He is, of course, immortalized in the Raffles Hotel. In the 20th century Singapore became the British imperial naval base in the Far East and, during the 1930s, it became a byword for arrogance and excess. Read J. G. Farrell's *The Singapore Grip*. After a shaming British defeat in World War II and the end of the empire, Singapore became a wretchedly poor but independent nation with apparently little going for it. At first, it almost became a part of Malaysia. From this extremely unpromising kick-off, with no natural resources, no industry

Singapore, 1941;
Singapore, 2010.

apart from a decaying dockyard, Singapore has emerged so that it now has an influential and admired place in the world. It is an astonishing achievement.

The vision of its authoritarian first leader, Lee Kuan Yew, has had a massive impact. He apparently said on 12 September 1965: *'Over 100 years ago, this was a mud-flat, swamp. Today, this is a modern city. Ten years from now, this will be a metropolis. Never fear.'*[1] And he was right. It was.

Lee Kuan Yew was Singapore's Atatürk. He knew what he wanted and he knew what he was doing. And he knew how he wanted the people of Singapore to behave. Singapore is now a highly individual place with a clear personality. It has a daunting work ethic and self-discipline which manifests itself in everything, from the behaviour of traffic to the way people use litter bins. Singapore is very recognizably Singaporean. It's not monolingual, although most Singaporeans speak Singlish, but many also speak their birth language, such as Mandarin or another Chinese language, Tamil, Hindi or Malay. Although the dominant ethnic group is Chinese, there are minorities of Indians, Malays, both from Malaysia and Indonesia, and plenty of Europeans, English and others – many of whom think of themselves as Singaporean.

The only Singaporean brand that the world knows is Singapore Airlines, until very recently the globally admired model in its field. But Singapore is also a major financial hub, a base for some massive companies in property, technology and many other areas of activity. It's the Asian home to Insead, one of the world's best-known business schools, and it's genuinely a knowledge centre with a number of major universities and world-class research institutes. It has a defence force, which is,

I am told, extremely potent for its size. In a word, Singapore is serious. Whatever Singapore does, it does with a daunting efficiency and thoroughness that makes German *Tüchtigkeit* look like sloth. I can't imagine anyone wanting to spend much time holidaying there, however, even though it's trying hard to be jolly and charming. For me, Singapore doesn't spell fun.

Singapore's real strength is that, through hard work, determination and a clear idea, it has made itself one of the major centres of the region. It was built around one man's vision. He saw an opportunity and he created a modern city state, the leading South East Asian city state. It has plenty of competition, of course. Hong Kong is also a city state of a kind and so is Shanghai, which is coming up to compete very fast. But all three of these places can probably live with each other because they recognize the existence of each other's strengths and, somehow, they are complementary to and even supportive of the others – a cluster. Theirs is a new place-branded world created because of opportunities in globalization.

• • •

There is also another group of place brands – in the Middle East: new, small place brands that have become very influential because they are rich and they sit on or have access to vast natural resources. In the Gulf there's Kuwait, Bahrain, Qatar, the United Arab Emirates (that is, Abu Dhabi, Dubai and a number of others): all places with tiny indigenous populations, lots of visitors and workers from other countries, and enormous wealth.

Some of them deploy sovereign investment funds, based on this wealth, which enables them to buy into strategic chunks of global business, giving them an influence way beyond their size. Dubai's Ports World is one of the three largest operators of sea ports and terminal cargo ports around the world: it has bases in the Middle East, Latin America, Europe, Asia and the United States. DP World helps make Dubai important and influential.

The state is also trying to turn itself into a holiday destination, with some apparent success. It has beaches, some man-made, and it has souks skilfully devised to look authentic. It has about seventy shopping malls, probably the highest density in the world; great, if you like that kind of thing. And it also has, of course, horse racing (Dubai's rulers are horse-crazy). It has some of the world's most extravagantly luxurious hotels; Dubai has been called the capital of bling. Perhaps most important of all, it has, like Singapore, an airport that's the regional hub. In addition, its airline, Emirates, is growing very fast and has a very good reputation, even now challenging Singapore Airlines as the world's most admired airline model. Dubai also seized an opportunity, had an idea and pursued it.

Other place brands in the region have a different emphasis. Qatar, right in the middle of the Gulf, has a population of about two million; its capital, Doha, around half a million. Even by city state standards, it's tiny. But it's extremely wealthy and is a significant regional, political and even military power. Its influence is everywhere. Through its various investment arms it owns the London department store Harrods, and it also happens to be the largest shareholder in Barclays Bank, and is a sponsor of the Barcelona Football Club – and that's just for starters. In fact, there isn't much that it doesn't do or isn't involved in. Qatar, a place that was virtually unknown until the last quarter of the 20th century, now has a considerable global weight – in politics, finance, academia, culture and even sport: in 2022 it will host the World Cup soccer tournament.

It is clear that the Qatar brand has been carefully thought through. Politically, Qatar leads the region. It has a moderate political stance, even though its leadership is strictly Muslim. Within a single generation, through brilliant brand development, it has become a political and cultural powerhouse. Through the sponsoring of Al-Jazeera, the broadcasting network, Qatar has created a platform as the pre-eminent reasonable and intelligent voice in the Middle East. Al-Jazeera has stature, and that stature reflects well on Qatar. It gives the state a gravitas and an influence that separates and distinguishes it from its neighbours. Al-Jazeera has been a political as well as a cultural triumph. Qatar is arguably the most intriguing and exciting example of the new place branding. It has come from nowhere inside a generation.

There was no serendipity. It wasn't an accident. There was an idea, a vision and the drive to do it. In the case of Singapore and Dubai, it was based around a transport hub but it has become much more. Qatar is different – a much bigger, bolder brand idea to become a significant political influence regionally and noticeable globally. And it has worked. Of course, wealth played a huge part. But it was the idea that made it happen.

•••

Finally, there are those place brands that have, quite unlike Singapore or Qatar, emerged largely through serendipity, through opportunity and accident. There was no Big Idea, no single driving force, although there were lots of people who, at different times in history, saw a chance and took it. These cities are so significant on the world stage that they have a life and an influence which is seen to be separate from the nation that they come from.

The classic example of this is London. London is a world city; maybe *the* world city. It depends on the world for its prosperity, and it is truly global. Home-grown British financial institutions in London are a tiny proportion of the whole; they are outsized and outranked by those from the United States, Europe and of course, increasingly, Asia. The London financial world doesn't just welcome foreign institutions; it depends on them.

In academia the story is similar. London has some of the world's most famous, most highly regarded universities. UCL, Imperial College, London School of Economics, Kings London are based in the city, and there are plenty more. Some of London's universities have up to 50% of foreign students among their population.

London is also arguably the world's centre for the creative industries. This doesn't imply that Londoners are necessarily especially creative; its creative industries are in fact full of brilliant Latin Americans, French, Indians and Russians and others, who find far more opportunities in London than they do in their home countries. London is an extraordinary cultural and creative powerhouse. It lives, as it always has, on immigration. It is a magnet for money, culture, creativity and even, perhaps surprisingly, with the Olympics, for sport.

London is lucky in some ways. Its time zone fits neatly between West and East, its working language is English, it has a reasonable rule of law, an exciting cultural scene, a temperate climate and, through good fortune, from time to time, some thoughtful and wise management and a history of looking at the world as a whole. That is why it has carved out a special place for itself. To survive, London has to be global; it can't depend on Britain.

London is always bracketed with New York. And New York and London do have a lot in common. They are about the same size in terms of population; they are both global financial, cultural and creative centres; they are both world tourist attractions; and they both have massive ethnic minorities. What's more, their main language is English, which makes them readily accessible to external influences. And that is where the resemblance ends.

New York is a great city but it's American and it depends on the United States. So, despite its vigour, charm and influence, it's not a global city brand. You can argue about how British or English London is. In my view, speaking as a Londoner, London is about London. It is part of, but different from, the rest of the UK.

• • •

Today, because of globalization, place brands can emerge from almost anywhere. A place brand can be a nation or a region or a city. A place brand can be very big, like China, or tiny, like Qatar. A place brand can be completely independent, like Singapore, or it can be part of somewhere else, like London. A place brand can be part of a country, a region, like Lombardy in northern Italy, or it can be composed of bits of several countries, like the Alpine or Baltic regions. There's a very high level of volatility in place branding. Some nations feel they are too small to be noticed so they cozy up to their neighbours; some cities feel they have something different, bigger and quite distinct from the nations they are part of; some regions may feel they have more in common with similar regions in other countries than they have with the nation of which they form a part. And, all of this, one way or another, is place branding. But what this is all about is seizing opportunity.

So, how does a place brand happen? There are, I think, four main factors which, coming together, often lead to the creation of the modern place brand. These are Opportunity, Personality, Credibility and Serendipity; and there's one other – Idea – which can be, but isn't always, a key element.

1. Opportunity

There are still plenty of opportunities around if you choose to look for them. Both Singapore and Dubai have grown into major regional transport hubs, because they saw an opportunity and seized it. Are there any opportunities like that left? Or have they all been grabbed – and it's all over? I think not.

Look at Latin America. Everyone tells us that Latin America is the next big opportunity, that everything is growing fast, that Colombia is now a haven of peace and tranquility, that Brazil is the B in the BRICS – and it's all true; well, more or less, true. But where is the regional air transport hub for Latin America? It's not in any country in Latin America; not in Colombia, not in Mexico, certainly not in Brazil. It's in Miami – Miami in the United States. So, there's an opportunity staring some Latin American city or nation in the face. That's just one opportunity. There are lots more – in Central and Eastern Europe, for instance.

There are also massive opportunities in soft power; that is, in political and cultural and humanitarian influence, when it's used with intelligence and discretion. Perhaps the most interesting current manifestation of this in broadcasting is Al-Jazeera, but there are plenty more where this came from. Of course, Deutsche Welle, Russia Today and a few other channels exist and they are trying hard – but perhaps not hard enough. They have seen the opportunity but they lack the personality and the credibility.

2. Personality

All truly great place brands have personality. They are immediately recognizable; you can close your eyes and visualize them. This isn't just because some dramatic visual feature can be symbolized – although sometimes there is one – but because they express a clear idea. Singapore is about efficiency; Dubai is about money.

When you have a personality, it shows. Any successful place brand has a personality we can relate to: Barcelona, Vienna, San Francisco, New Orleans, Florence. We can see them with our mind's eye. But Phuket, Torremolinos, almost anywhere in Florida – I am not so sure.

How can you distinguish many tourist destinations from each other, especially hot, sunny, sandy ones? Of course, not all hot and sunny places are the same. The French Riviera isn't like the Costa del Sol, which is just a few hundred miles away. But wherever developers have been allowed to do what they wanted, they have ignored everything except cost, which means that they have built what will in time become anonymous seaside slums, impossible to tell apart – and it shows. The tourist advertising for Morocco, Mexico, Thailand and nearly every other hot, sunny country is similar because tourist organizations have turned their holiday destinations into commodities, literally package tours, and they have ignored or didn't understand the personality of the country they were dealing with. Over time, these places, built in a rush by too-greedy developers, will rot quietly in the sun, while holiday-makers find places with more local charm and style.

3. Credibility

Remember who you are, where you are, what you are and what your strengths (and weaknesses) are. Do not pretend to be what you are not. There is only one Silicon Valley ... and it's in California; it's not in Romania, or Latvia, or Portugal.

4. Serendipity

Being in the right place at the right time with the right product mix: London, maybe, is the classic example. London has grown into its pre-eminent position because various astute people have at different times seen an opportunity and grabbed it. There was never a master plan, and there isn't one now. Nor, I suspect, will there ever be. London has never had an Atatürk or a Lee Kuan Yew (although some of its mayors might like to think they are).

Silicon Valley is another example of serendipity. Nobody planned it. A combination of brilliant young people, the focus of Stanford University and an entrepreneurial business climate came together and it just started to happen.

This kind of unplanned flowering will happen increasingly. The opportunities for place brands to emerge in unlikely ways from unlikely places and become significant players on a global stage are getting bigger as the world gets better connected.

Of course, if you want to be a transport hub, it matters where you are; otherwise, not so much. Place brands in finance, technology, tourism, education, creativity and everything else you can think of will flourish whether they are in Stockholm or Santiago – if they have something special to offer.

Just occasionally, very rarely, a place brand is based around an idea. Atatürk in Turkey, the Al-Thani family in Qatar and Lee Kuan Yew in Singapore: all had an idea and built extraordinary powerful and built-to-last brands around it. There's a lot to go for.

Afterword.
A Few Thoughts.

On My Career

Few of us who were at university in the 1950s in Britain had any clear idea of what we wanted to do afterwards, unless we were studying for a vocation, like medicine. Nor did we get much help. There was a careers office which handed out bits of paper with the vaguest platitudes about possible jobs.

The options seemed to be: the Civil Service, if you wanted to be safe, although it wasn't always that safe (one of my friends thought he was joining the Foreign Office and became a spy instead). Or, if you fancied a career in industry, there was Shell, Unilever, ICI and a few other big companies. If you thought you were a bit creative, there was the BBC. And that was about it, unless there was a family firm knocking about somewhere in the background. A few people became actors or freelance journalists or writers. Nobody really even dreamed that they could start a business on their own – from scratch. 'Start your own business? Doing what? Are you crazy?'

I felt I had a creative streak and I could clown around a bit, make people laugh, and write a little, but I didn't think that with my third-class honours degree in history I would get into the BBC. So my career was stalled before I had even started.

Then came some kind of an epiphany. I went to the cinema one evening and saw an English film called *Genevieve*, about an old car rally from London to Brighton. The hero wore a fancy waistcoat, took lots of pretty girls to lunch, seemed well-off, owned a greatly admired veteran car (they were called 'old crocks' then), apparently had plenty of time for leisure activities, and he had a job – although he didn't seem to work much – in advertising. I fell for the whole thing at once.

I wrote to a lot of advertising agencies, had a few interviews and took the first job I was offered. So that's how, in my characteristically well-thought-through fashion, I chose my career.

In those days, and for quite a long time afterwards, advertising agencies were the lead suppliers of every kind of communication advice and activity to their clients. In addition to conventional advertising in the press, cinemas, television, hoardings and so on, they looked after almost everything else in the communication world. The design of packaging, logos, exhibition stands was either carried out internally or sub-contracted to small graphic design studios. Agencies also monitored everything else from PR to market research. I found it a thrilling learning experience and I became involved in most of the kinds of work that the agency did.

After a few short and exciting years in the London agency (it was 'Mad Men' time), I asked to go to New York, where my firm had partnered another London company, to back David Ogilvy. My boss said, 'They don't know anything about advertising in New York. Go to Bombay instead.' So that's how I went to India. And a couple of years after I arrived in Bombay I was put in charge of our Indian operations. And it was only when I became CEO of the company that's now called Ogilvy in India that I began to sense the boundaries of the advertising world.

Ogilvy (or Benson as it was then called) had quite a big business in India and I travelled all the time all over the country. I developed an addiction for India that I have never lost. Whenever I arrive at Mumbai airport, even today, that very particular smell – a mix of jasmine and shit – brings it all back.

We had clients in fast moving consumer goods, fertilisers, airlines, perfumes, clothing, hotels, animal and human health; all kinds of things. We worked for foreign companies and Indian companies – especially some of the Tata companies. But they were all in the private sector.

At that time, the early 1960s, India, under Prime Minister Jawaharlal Nehru and his successors, was a Socialist state, very keen on self-development through vast public corporations which dominated the economy. Some of us in the advertising business tried, and mostly failed, to get work from some of these huge state organizations. But that's how I came to visit two state steel plants, one run with German co-operation and the other dominated by the Soviets.

I was, perhaps naively, amazed at how different the plants were from one another. They both made steel but, apart from that, they couldn't have been more different. The way the offices looked, the working environments, the behaviour of people at levels both to each other and to the world outside, and of course, as part of all that, their communications, were completely different from each other. They were separate, isolated worlds, in personality, in charm (or lack of it), in the way they felt about themselves.

From a business point of view both trips were a complete waste of time. The plants were secretive and neither thought we had anything to contribute, but I became very intrigued by steel. So, partly because I was interested, but also because I had good connections with some Tata businesses, I arranged a trip to the Tata Iron and Steel Company (Tisco) at Jamshedpur in what was then Bihar, at the time one of India's poorest and most lawless states, to see if we could do anything with them.

Tata had set up the steel plant in around 1907. It was the first in India – and the most admired. Jamshedpur, founded by Jamshedji Tata, was almost a model town, and the way Tata people behaved, combined with the environment at the site – it was green and clean and welcoming, and the people were properly proud of it – made a huge impact on me. It couldn't have been more different from the two state steel works. Tisco didn't try to sell steel through advertising, of course, but the entire place, because it was so surprisingly clean, co-ordinated, orderly and well-maintained, sold the product. Jamshedpur was impressive. Somehow you knew they made good stuff.

Those three visits had a long-term impact on the way I thought about companies. How could three organizations, making more or less the same product, in more or less the same way, be so startlingly unlike each other?

That is, looking back on it, when I began for the first time to sense that a corporation communicates what it is through everything it does; that advertising is at most only a small part of it. I began to feel that there must be a broader, more comprehensive way of presenting an organization to its various worlds. And that idea has been driving my career, often subconsciously, one way or another, ever since.

On Corporate Identity

When I came back to the UK, I left advertising and, after a few vicissitudes, looked around for another way of earning a living. I came across and into the world of graphic design. I was not, of course, a designer but I loved the design world and it seemed to be changing ... fast. Eminent designers both in Europe and the United States were developing co-ordinated visual identity programmes with large and often influential clients. They had been doing this for many years, and I've written about it elsewhere, but the scene was just beginning to change.

Many high-minded organizations, such as London Transport, Olivetti in Italy, and IBM, Mobil and Container Corporation in the United States, had been working on major visual identity programmes that co-ordinated their design output in products, environments and communications, but, during the 1960s, visual identity began to reach further into the corporation. The original intention, which was to project a unified corporate face, became part of the process by which the company attempted to differentiate itself and its products from its competitors, and even to market itself to the outside world.

I joined with Michael Wolff, a young and brilliant creative director whom I also met entirely by chance, to start Wolff

Michael Wolff (left),
Wally Olins (right) and
dustbins. Wolff Olins,
1960s.

Olins in London, one of the design consultancies groping its way towards developing this kind of activity. Of course graphic design was the core of our business and, under Michael's inspiration, our company produced some startlingly original and successful work. And then we began to grow in a piecemeal and haphazard kind of way. We would be commissioned to design some packaging or an exhibition stand for a large corporation. It sometimes emerged, as we started the work, that our client owned many companies which had been acquired at different times, independently of each other. So we often came across corporations with a multiplicity of half-absorbed brands, each with its own name and visual identity, taken over in a piecemeal fashion.

When, during the course of our work, we presented this overlapping shambles, or what we preferred to call this 'uncontrolled visual identity' to our clients, their senior people often recognized the issue and we were sometimes commissioned to help sort it out. And that's how, in my observation, what we now call 'brand architecture' began to develop. We also began to get programmes for smaller companies that wanted to stand out visually from their competitors, and from companies merging with each other, who were looking for a new name and identity. For each of these, when we had an opportunity, we developed an identity strategy and a visual identity based around it.

From the graphic design base that dominated our early years, we gradually, opportunistically, haphazardly morphed into a corporate identity consultancy that looked at the personality, core idea and brand architecture of our clients' businesses and projected it, initially visually. And we carried out research. Well, anyway, we talked to people inside and outside the company.

The first time we worked for a bank (it was quite a small bank; they had small banks then), we thought it would be about right to interview 10% of the branch managers: sixty people. After the first five or six interviews we had a pretty clear idea about what the remaining fifty-five would say. And that's how we learned how to take what was subsequently called 'a statistically significant sample'.

Did we actually know what we were doing? Yes, I'm sure we did, intuitively. We learned a lot from every job we did. As we carried out more work, we became more experienced, more confident and bolder. And the visual work that Michael's team created was striking, groundbreaking and commercially successful.

As we did more investigation and talked to people inside the organization, we discovered how little very many people knew about the company they were working for. I remember sitting with the driver of a Lever Sunlicht truck in Hamburg. We talked about working for a non-German company and I asked

him who owned Lever Sunlicht. Unilever, he said. So I asked
who owned Unilever. He said he wasn't quite sure but he'd been
told that it was owned by the Queen of England and the Queen
of the Netherlands! So that's the kind of thing that led to the
introduction and development of what we now call 'internal
engagement programmes'.

Of course, we looked closely at the personality of the
companies we were working for. The experience with the three
Indian steel companies was always in the back of my mind. What
made companies different from one another? It's tempting, with
hindsight, to rationalize and claim that we had a clear objective
and knew where we were going. But it wasn't quite like that.
We knew we were on to something but we weren't quite sure
what it was. We were not alone. Many of our competitors were
in the same position.

As the nature of our work expanded, we recruited people from
different backgrounds and disciplines. In addition to our core of
graphic designers, we took on strategy consultants, architects,
writers, PR and HR people and, by the time I was commissioned
to write a book in 1976, we were able to talk and write about 'the
corporate personality' with some authority.

In *The Corporate Personality* I tried to examine why companies
used the tools of corporate identity, and I looked at the
difference between the corporation and its brands. I looked at
the different personalities of a variety of different companies.
I looked at mergers and takeovers and why they succeeded
and why they failed. I wrote about names and naming. I even
used the 'brand' word a bit. I also wrote about nations and the
national brand, which has always fascinated me. Why did some
former African colonies create new names when they became

independent? Why did East Pakistan, after it broke away from West Pakistan, call itself Bangladesh? What is a nation anyway? What is a national identity? Like most of my subsequent books it had an historical, sociological and anthropological as well as design and business emphasis.

Gradually, we – all those identity consultancies in London, New York and a few other places – found that we had opened up a new commercial activity. And, as it grew up, like so many other industries, it rebranded itself. Corporate identity became branding.

On Branding Growing Up

Very rapidly, virtually overnight, in the mid- to late 1980s, the branding consultancy activity took off and matured into a complex and high-profile business. The big communication conglomerates, like WPP and Omnicom, saw branding as a business opportunity. They could see that the brand could be the centre of their clients' businesses. They bought up some of the independent boutiques and, through mergers around the world, created a few big global consultancies who professionalized the business very effectively. These consultancies talked and wrote about the financial value of the brand and they influenced clients to make branding a central activity.

The new bigger brand consultancies brought a gloss and sophistication to the business, especially because they emphasized the financial muscle of brands and branding. They introduced a new methodology that made the process of branding look complicated, purposeful, professional and perhaps above all fool-proof. They relied deeply on process and system; on head rather than heart.

The new branding programmes seemed to reduce the possibility of chance and error; they seemed to turn branding from a creative art to a science; they appeared to be able to reduce risk and, therefore, to justify expenditure. Over a quite short period, the corporate world came to understand that brands were a valuable financial asset to be nurtured and cherished for the longer-term health of the business. They were taught that brands mean profit and share price, and they 'add value'.

Today nobody doubts that brands are really important. As we have seen, they are rated in a pecking order according to their purported financial value, and brand managers are persuaded to be confident that if they spend millions they will earn billions. The branding activity has become ubiquitous. There's hardly a nation in the world that doesn't have brand consultancies and that isn't developing brands.

On Management Schools

Around the last quarter of the 20th century branding became a fashionable subject in business and management schools. A small number of clever academics wrote thoughtful and comprehensive books about branding and they began to systematize it and construct a discipline around the brand world. This gave branding a new status and position within management thinking. Complex studies were written about every conceivable facet of branding: emotional factors, rational factors, empathy in luxury products, different kinds of brand strategy in products and services. They created a formidable quota of words and phrases around brand platforms, brand values, brand endorsements, brand architecture, brand extension and almost everything else you can think of.

Branding began to be taught in business schools, sometimes as part of marketing and sometimes as a quasi-distinct activity. Now there's a plethora of academic journals devoted to every conceivable aspect of the subject, and all of this leads to methodologies of mind-boggling complexity. Put another way, because branding is now seen to be a precious long-term asset of considerable and in some cases (e.g. Virgin, Coca-Cola) overwhelming financial value, it has arrived at the centre both of the business and management school syllabus.

Somewhat to my initial surprise, I was invited to join the management academic community. I've lectured at quite a few business schools around the world. To my amusement, I am sometimes called 'Professor'.

On Branding: Simple or Sinister

It is perhaps curious, with all these levels of hyperactivity around branding, that it's still the subject of so much misunderstanding and even disdain.

There's the simplistic view, which is quite common: for many people branding is just a logo. 'So you do logos, do you? I like that Nike one.' I was told not long ago by a quite serious executive that a brand is a label, sometimes with a slogan attached. So what is all the fuss about? It's not surprising that people inside corporations who take that view are likely to treat brand as a subordinate adjunct to advertising. 'Get the agency creatives to bash out a couple of logos and we'll choose one. We shouldn't have to pay for it. They earn enough off us already.'

Then there's another attitude towards brands and branding which is right at the other end of the spectrum. The word 'brand' is associated with everything that is cosmetic, superficial and phoney. Naomi Klein's *No Logo*, which is an attack on the behaviour of big business, exemplifies this view. The logo, the brand if you like, is the symbol and visible manifestation of the manipulative, deceitful corporation. The logo and its brand are the disingenuous gloss that the corporation uses to cover up its malign activities.

Since I call myself a brand consultant, I am not unnaturally curious about this. I find it all the more strange since 'reputation' and 'identity', which have similar meanings, are perfectly OK words. 'Reputation', particularly, has implications of trust and value. If I talk about reputation at an academic conference, the audience nods gravely but if I mention 'brand', some people in the audience get visibly queasy. So what's the big difference? It seems to me that at least part of the reason why the word 'brand' attracts disdain in some quarters is that it's associated with campaigns, particularly with advertising campaigns.

On Long-Term vs Short-Term

As I hope I've made clear in this book, I truly believe that the powerful, effective brand is about authenticity and, when you try to fake it, as many organizations do, it shows. And you have to stay with the brand for the long term. It has to stand for something real. Of course you can modulate the brand so that it is appropriate for different audiences, and it has to evolve and change with mutating circumstances, but in the end, in my view, the brand essence is permanent and must remain stable. The brand must be clearly, recognizably authentic wherever and however it's used.

And, of course, this raises big issues. With digital media, for example, the corporation and its brands and its audiences get much closer to each other than ever before and digital advertising on websites, mobile devices and so on is the big growth area. The strength of such advertising is that it can be aimed directly at a specific target audience at a particular moment, and it's very often possible to gauge the impact on sales of one particular spot. So it seems that at last, after about 150 years, it may be possible to bring some kind of precision to advertising. That's why advertisers love it. Digital advertising has extraordinary short-term power. 'With new digital tools marketers can reach the likeliest customers when they are more in the mood to buy,' noted *The Economist.*[1] And that may mean that, in the interests of short-term impact and a high rate of hits, some advertisers may get carried away by tactics and forget about the core idea of the brand.

I genuinely believe that there is a real danger of damaging the long-term brand strategy if you strive too hard for immediate tactical success with a short-term fix which is off-brand. On the other hand, in a situation which presents an opportunity – an unexpected sporting victory, a celebrity wedding, or something similar – the opportunity to exploit the strength of the brand for the occasion should be unmissable. This is the moment to underline brand strengths, not to ignore them, but it means thinking a bit harder and longer.

Contrary to what many experts seem to believe, digital isn't killing the brand. In fact, I think the digital age brings greater opportunities for brands and branding than ever before. Digital can bring the brand to its audience with much more impact and immediacy than ever before. The brand has never had this opportunity to be so close to the consumer. We consumers still love the intimacy of the brand as well as its spontaneity and adaptability.

On What I Believe About the Brand

For me branding isn't just an important tool in the communication business. It is a fundamental manifestation of the human condition. It is about knowing who you are, having a sense of your own individuality and of where you belong, and showing it. Whether this relates to a person or a nation or a product, it makes no difference.

Without a sense of belonging and without demonstrating a sense of belonging and without eliciting the reactions of others, we wouldn't – for better or worse – be what we are.

A Few Things I Have Learned

I've been about fifty years in the business of branding and, together with some of my colleagues, I've played a small part in the process of growing and shaping the branding activity. So I thought it might be permissible for me to try and make a few observations summing up some of the things I may have learned and how it's all going:

- However good an organization looks from a distance, the closer you get, the more flaws and weaknesses you see. When you get near enough, you find there are no good organizations. Internal politics, poor communication, bureaucracy and petty-mindedness exist absolutely everywhere.
- Where there's strong, committed leadership, a branding programme will take root and become an intrinsic part of the institutional fabric. Where there isn't, it will gradually disintegrate and all the organization will be left with is an empty shell.

- There's no such thing as a merger of equals. When one organization merges with another, there's always a winner and a loser.
- I've worked in three sectors: politics, as an adviser to national and regional governments and cities; academia, both as a consultant to academic institutions and universities and as an academic, inside them; and business, as a consultant to large and small companies in many countries. I've also worked as a small-time entrepreneur. On balance, although each has its charm, I find business the least difficult arena to work in. There's (usually) a clear chain of command, there's a goal, a target and measurable objectives, so after a bit you know if you're achieving them. Politicians and academics are generally much more vague and the internal politics is sometimes even worse.
- IQ is beating EQ. Right now in the permanent struggle between analytics and intuition, data is winning. But the wheel will turn. It always does.
- Facebook, Twitter, texts and all the technology will not replace human contact. You can't have family Christmas dinner on Skype.
- Branding is getting too complex. The way branding is taught in business schools and the manner in which it's mostly practised is unnecessarily complicated. Don't let process drive it. Fundamentally, branding is easy to understand. Don't make it so difficult.
- Great symbols – logos, the visual manifestations of the brand – tug at the heartstrings. That's why national flags and religious symbols still have such immense power.
- Never underestimate the gap between national cultures.

- Don't fake it. It always shows in the end.
- Don't ever break trust.
- Be authentic.
- Corporate social responsibility isn't window dressing. It's an intrinsic part of what the corporation does, or should do.
- The more the world homogenizes and globalizes the more it provokes and inspires heterogeneity and individuality. That's why creativity in branding will continue to flourish.
- You can learn much more from things that go wrong than from things that go right.
- Oh, and one more thing. I've had fifty years of poking my nose into other people's business … and I've enjoyed it; not all the time, but most of it.

- **Have fun**!

Notes

Chapter 1. The New Authenticity

1   As I was writing this chapter, I happened to glance at a copy of a UK newspaper, the *Daily Mail* (4 July 2012). The headline read: 'Banned, Special K advert that misled viewers over calories'. It appears that the copy on the Kellogg's Special K cereal packaging was misleading. The cereal actually contained more sugar than its competitors. Not much of a surprise there....

2   See 'Prada's new range is made in heaven' by Tamsin Blanchard, *The Daily Telegraph*, 22 October 2010: http://fashion.telegraph.co.uk/news-features/TMG8081394/Pradas-new-range-is-made-in-heaven.html.

3   'The Global Nutrition Environment Workplace Goal', published by Pepsi, 2008.

Chapter 2. Corporate Confusion

1   *The Machine Age in America: 1918–1941* by Richard Guy Wilson, Dianne H. Pilgrim and Dickran Tashjian, Brooklyn Museum of Art and Harry N. Abrams, 1986.

2   *The Economist*, 26 January 2013.

3   *The Guardian*, 21 December 2012.

4   'Why No One's Listening to a Walkman' by Gillian Tett, *FT Magazine*, 18 January 2013.

5   Personal correspondence to the author from Ian Stephens.

Chapter 3. Dealing with the New Zeitgeist

1   http://www.telegraph.co.uk/news/aviation/9490368/Woman-forced-to-pay-200-to-print-out-Ryanair-tickets.html.

2   'SITA Stats Confirm Ryanair is No. 1 with Fewest Mishandled Bags', Ryanair press release, 29 May 2012.

3   http://www.theguardian.com/business/2006/oct/26/theairlineindustry.lifeandhealth.

4   http://www.telegraph.co.uk/travel/travelnews/10127013/Ryanair-still-the-worlds-favourite-airline.html.

5   'Global Powers of Retailing 2013: Retail Perspectives from Deloitte', report, 18 February 2012, p. 10.

6   http://www.retail-week.com/home/profile-tesco-the-uks-largest-retailer/5046179.article.

7   *The Guardian*, 18 February 2013.

8   *The Economist*, 23 February 2013.

9   BBC News, December 2012.

10 Joseph Tripodi, in a speech to an industry audience at the Cannes Lions International Festival of Creativity, quoted in *The Guardian*, 21 June 2013.

Chapter 5. Big Brand Takes Over (or Doesn't)

1   *Sunday Observer*, 5 May 2013.

2   *The Economist*, 29 June 2013.

3   *Ibid.*

4   See 'How A Young Community Of Entrepreneurs Is Rebuilding Detroit' by

Chuck Salter: http://www.
fastcompany.com/3007840/
creative-conversations/
how-young-community-
entrepreneurs-rebuilding-
detroit.

5   'The Crowds That Shun the
Mass Market', *New York Times*,
10 June 2012.

6   Quoted from a full-page IBM
advertisement in *The Economist*,
15 June 2012.

7   *The Economist*, 18 May 2013.

8   *The Financial Times*, 3 May 2013.

9   Science & Technology section,
The Economist, 2 April 2011,
p. 86.

10   *Marketing Week*, 11 October 2012.

11   *The Guardian*, 11 January 2013.

12   *The Independent*, 17 November
2006.

**Chapter 6. New Brands From
Everywhere**

1   Introduction, *Encounters:
The Meeting of Asia and
Europe, 1500–1800*, ed. Anna
Jackson and Amin Jaffer,
V&A Publications, 2004.

2   *The Financial Times*, 27 August
2010.

3   *The Financial Times*, 21 March
2012.

4   'How To Spend It', *The Financial
Times*, 4 May 2013.

**Chapter 7. National Prosperity
and Nation Branding**

1   Eric Hobsbawm, *Nations
and Nationalism since 1780:
Programme, Myth, Reality*,
Cambridge University Press,
1992.

2   *New York Times*, 12 June 2011.

Chapter 8. Branding the Place

1   Lee Kuan Yew, quoted in an
advertisement for Temasek
Holdings in *The Economist*,
7 July 2012.

Afterword: A Few Thoughts

1   'Less Guff, More Puff',
The Economist, 30 July 2013.

Select Bibliography

For me a bibliography is about sources – books, of course, but also newspapers, film, television, the internet. I've been reading, listening and watching all my life so the selection here is just a small sample of material that has influenced me.

Books

Aaker, David, *Building Strong Brands*, Simon & Schuster, 2002

Ahmed, Mohi, and Marc Silvester, *Living Service: How to Deliver the Service of the Future Today*, FT Prentice Hall, 2008

Anderson, Benedict, *Imagined Communities: Reflections on the Origin and Spread of Nationalism*, Verso, 1983

Bacon, Edmund N., *Design of Cities*, rev. ed., Penguin, 1976

Banerjee, Abhijit, and Esther Duflo, *Poor Economics*, Penguin, 2012

Barton, Bruce, *The Man Nobody Knows*, Ivan R. Dee, 2000 (first pub. Bobbs-Merrill, 1925)

Bhat, Harish, *Tata Log*, Portfolio Penguin Books India, 2012

Bobbitt, Philip, *The Shield of Achilles: War, Peace and the Course of History*, Penguin, 2003

Cartwright, Justin, *Other People's Money*, Bloomsbury, 2012

Colley, Linda, *Britons Forging the Nation 1707–1837*, Pimlico, 1992

Davies, Norman, *Vanished Kingdoms: The History of Half-Forgotten Europe*, Penguin, 2012

Diamond, Jared, *Guns, Germs and Steel: A Short History of Everybody for the Last 13,000 Years*, Vintage, 1998

Farrell, J. G., *The Singapore Grip*, Phoenix, 1996

Fielding, Henry, *The History of Tom Jones, A Foundling*, A. Millar, 1749

Fisher, Mark, *Capitalism Realism: Is There No Alternative?*, Zero Books, 2009

Fombrun, Charles J., *Reputation: Realizing Value from the Corporate Image*, Harvard Business School Press, 1996

Friedman, Thomas L., *The World Is Flat: A Brief History of the Twenty-First Century*, Penguin, 2nd rev ed., 2007 (1st ed. Farrar, Straus and Giroux, 2005)

Garfield, Simon, *Just My Type: A Book About Fonts*, Gotham, 2012 (reprint)

Goldacre, Ben, *Bad Pharma: How Drug Companies Mislead Doctors and Harm Patients*, Fourth Estate, 2012

Hall, Peter, *Cities of Tomorrow: An Intellectual History of Urban Planning and Design in the Twentieth Century*, Wiley-Blackwell, 3rd ed., 2002

Harvey, David, *The Enigma of Capitalism*, Profile Books, 2011

Judt, Tony, and Timothy Snyder, *Thinking the Twentieth Century*, Vintage, 2013

Kahneman, Daniel, *Thinking, Fast and Slow*, Penguin, 2012

Kay, John, *Culture and Prosperity: The Truth about Markets. Why Some Nations Are Rich but Most Remain Poor*, Harper Business, 2003

——, *The Long and the Short of it: A Guide to Finance and Investment for Normally Intelligent People Who Aren't in the Industry*, Erasmus Press, 2009

—, *Obliquity: Why our Goals are Best Achieved Indirectly*, Profile Books, 2010

Kellaway, Lucy, *Who moved my Blackberry?*, Hyperion, 2006

Klein, Naomi, *No Logo*, Picador, 1999

Kleveman, Lutz, *The New Great Game: Blood and Oil in Central Asia*, Atlantic Books (new ed.), 2004

Lanchester, John, *Whoops! Why Everyone Owes Everyone and No-one Can Pay*, Penguin, 2010

—, *Capital*, Faber & Faber, 2013

Landes, David S., *Wealth and Poverty of Nations*, Abacus, 1999

Maass, Peter, *Crude World: The Violent Twilight of Oil*, Allen Lane, 2009

MacKenzie, John M., *Propaganda and Empire: The Manipulation of British Public Opinion*, Manchester University Press, 1984

Mango, Andrew, *Ataturk: The Biography of the Founder of Modern Turkey*, Overlook Press, 2002

Morgan, Nigel, Annette Pritchard, and Roger Pride, *Destination Branding: Creating the Unique Destination Proposition*, Butterworth-Heinemann, 2004

Pinker, Steven, *The Better Angels of Our Nature: A History of Violence and Humanity*, Penguin, 2012

Ridderstrale, Johnas, and Kjell Nordstrom, *Funky Business*, ft.com 2000

Roth, Joseph, *The Radetzky March*, Penguin Classics (new ed.), 2000

Schultz, Majken, Mary Jo Hatch, and Mogens Holten Larsen, *The Expressive Organization: Linking Identity, Reputation, and the Corporate Brand*, Oxford University Press, 2000

Schumpeter, Joseph, *Capitalism, Socialism and Democracy*, Harper, 1975

Sinclair, Upton, *The Jungle*, Dover Publications, 2001 (first pub. Doubleday, Jabber & Co., 1906)

Trollope, Anthony, *The Way We Live Now*, Wordsworth Classics, 1999 (first published Chapman & Hall, 1875)

Van Riel, Cees, *Principles of Corporate Communication*, Routledge, 2007

—, *The Alignment Factor: Leveraging the Power of Total Stakeholder Support*, Routledge, 2012

Wiedemann, Julius (ed.), *Logo Design*, Vol. 2, Taschen, 2009

Wilson, Richard Guy, Dianne H. Pilgrim, and Dickran Tashjian, *The Machine Age in America: 1918–1941*, Brooklyn Museum of Art and Harry N. Abrams (reprint), 2001

Yew, Lee Kuan, *From Third World to First: The Singapore Story 1965–2000. Singapore and the Asian Economic Boom*, Harper Collins, 2011

If you want to really understand Turkey, Orhan Pamuk is the best: *Istanbul: Memories of a City*, Faber & Faber, 2006; *The Museum of Innocence*, Faber & Faber, 2010; *My Name is Red*, Faber & Faber, 2011.

Zola, Balzac, Dickens and Trollope all gave business a bad time.

G. A. Henty, Sapper, John Buchan and Captain W. E. Johns all produced books at a time when the British took their superiority everywhere for granted. It's both amusing and embarrassing to read them now.

I've written quite a bit about branding in my life, so if you want to read more, these are my previous books: *The Corporate Personality: An Inquiry into the Nature of the Corporate Identity*, Mayflower Books, 1978; *Corporate Identity: Making Business Strategy Visible through Design*, Harvard Business School Press, 1990; *On Brand*, Thames & Hudson, 2003; *Wally Olins: The Brand Handbook*, Thames & Hudson, 2008.

Picture Credits

Newspapers and magazines

Financial Times, especially the columns by Lucy Kellaway, John Kay and Gillian Tett

The Economist

The Observer

Monocle Magazine

Films

Capitalism: A Love Story, by Michael Moore (2009)

Fast Food Nation: The Dark Side of the All-American Meal, by Eric Schlosser (2002)

Wall Street, by Oliver Stone (1987)

Money Never Sleeps, by Oliver Stone (2010)

TV

When you spend as much of your life in hotel rooms as I do, you have the opportunity to watch the world through other people's eyes. Apart from BBC World and CNBC, I usually learn a bit from Russia Today, Al Jazeera and Deutsche Welle.

p. 9 Saffron Brand Consultants Ltd

p. 13 Photo Andra Oprisan

p. 16 Courtesy Innocent Drinks

p. 51 Artist's impression by Rémy Auger

p. 57 Photo Andra Oprisan

p. 61 Private collection

p. 83 Mary Evans Picture Library

p. 97 Photos Andra Oprisan

p. 115 Mary Evans Picture Library

p. 128 (above) Courtsy Nissan Cars

p. 128 (below) © Getty Images News; photographer Feng Li

p. 139 (left) Courtesy Cavit Isici

p. 140 Photo Daren Cook

p. 141 Photo Andra Oprisan

p. 145 Photos Andra Oprisan

p. 158 © Getty Images/Archive Photos; photography Fotosearch

p. 164 (above) © Getty Images/ Time & Life Pictures; photographer Carl Mydans

p. 164 (below) Photo Daren Cook

p. 181 Wolff Olins Archive

Acknowledgments

I feel that I've been writing this book, or versions of it, most of my life and, of course, I've picked up ideas from all kinds of people in all kinds of different places over the years, so, inevitably, the list of acknowledgments will be partial, and if I've missed a few people – and I'm sure I have – it's because I forgot. Sorry.

At work in Saffron I'd like to thank my colleagues in London, Ian Stephens, Ben Knapp, Emma Booty, Isabela Chick, Sahil Sachdev, Inga Howell, Corinne Myers, Nick Sims, Wendy and Ian Roberts, and others who have put up with my wandering around the office mumbling to myself. They sometimes interrupted with some interesting thoughts. I thank Rémy Auger for his witty illustration of Ryanair passengers standing. In Madrid Jacob Benbunan, Gabor Schreier and many others inspired me. In Istanbul, Turgay Adiyaman always has a lively, useful angle. India excites, inspires and infuriates me in more or less equal parts, so thank you very much Bobby Sista and Rajesh Kejriwal.

My very good friend and client, Mohi Ahmed, has made me think hard; we've worked up a few ideas together. Thank you, Mohi.

I have to thank both Andra Oprisan, my research assistant, and Liz Queenan, my PA, especially. I must at times have driven them quite crazy. Type it. Re-type it. 'Are you sure you've got that right? I can't quite believe that. It doesn't sound right. Check it again.' Thank you so much both of you for putting up with me.

And finally there's Daren Cook, who designed the book. He just took the typescript and understood better than I did how it should look and feel on paper. 'No, don't have too many illustrations. It won't work like that. It isn't a picture book.' And I took his advice and then he did it. Brilliantly, as always.

Thank you, all of you. And thank you, Dornie.

Index

Figures in *italic* refer to illustrations